The Smile on My Forehead:
Memoir of My Life
With a Brain Injury

The Smile on My Forehead: Memoir of My Life With a Brain Injury

Jennifer Mosher

Disclaimer: The effects of my Traumatic Brain Injury are uniquely mine and this memoir is not intended to professionally advise TBI Survivors or their families.

Contents

Acknowledgements

Writing is a process and very often a manuscript's final draft barely resembles the first. As this is the case with me, I'd like to thank the following people for their help in my process.

Deirdre Paulsen, my Writing Fellows director at BYU, for asking me, "Have you written your story yet?"

Colleen Whitley, the Co-director of BYU Publication Lab, for being so willing to help after meeting me only once, and the students in the BYU Publication Lab who read my early drafts.

Janet Garrard-Willis, another Writing Fellow and my friend, for her masterful edits.

Britta Nelson for suggesting I join the League of Utah Writers, and for a wonderful friendship.

Marsha Lundgren and **Robin Pratt** at the League of Utah Writers for reading my first complete draft.

Fritz McDonald at the University of Iowa Summer Writing Festival for helping me to shape my memoir.

Dr. Tom White and all other medical staff who took care of me at Regional West Medical Center in Nebraska, thank you for saving my life.

The biggest thank you to my family for constantly supporting me, both before and after my life with a brain injury.

Foreword

I met Jennifer Mosher after an ambulance rushed her into the Level II Trauma Center at Regional West Medical Center in Scottsbluff, Nebraska. She lay on an Emergency Department gurney, fully "packaged," strapped to a hard backboard, shattered legs in splints, and in deep coma. Critically injured in a car accident, she clung to life.

As a trauma surgeon, I'd seen this situation a dozen times before, and a hundred times since. The initial evaluation of my patients is always fast-paced, rigorous, and my thoughts often drift. I wonder: *What was this person like? What will happen to them if they survive?* Jennifer's remarkable recovery and her eloquent story telling have afforded me a rare opportunity to have these questions answered.

Traumatic brain injury affects an estimated 1.4 million Americans each year. Approximately 230,000 are hospitalized and 30,000 die. Although it's the leading cause of disability following a traumatic injury, its repercussions are not completely understood. Victims who are injured as severely as Jennifer often don't survive, and if they do they have significant long-term disability. As a medical community, we aren't good at predicting how individual patients will ultimately fare, which makes initial treatment decisions challenging.

Occasionally a patient with severe brain injury will make a miraculous recovery. Jennifer is just such a patient. She struggles daily with fatigue, memory loss, and attention because the injury has disrupted her brain's circuitry, which has undergone a re-routing, and simply isn't as efficient anymore. She compensates remarkably well, and only her closest friends and family would suspect anything out of the ordinary.

Jennifer's story serves as inspiration to the many who have survived, and those who live with or care for someone with Traumatic Brain Injury. Her recovery reminds me of why we, as trauma healthcare providers, do what we do.

She and I meet regularly now, usually at a busy restaurant with our families. We inevitably talk about her ordeal, but the conversation quickly moves to more mundane topics such as family, movies, or writing. Fourteen years ago I felt proud and privileged to be her doctor. Now, I'm delighted just to be her friend.

Thomas W. White, M.D., FACS
Trauma Surgery and Critical Care
Salt Lake City, Utah
November 2007

Preface

I feel like an inchworm trying to write a book. Each time I pull out my notes to work, I think of a great idea and inch forward in my writing. But, then I become distracted because I look out the window, or think about something entirely unrelated to my story. Once I reel myself back in, I can't even remember what my idea was in the first place, so I reread what I've already written, hoping to find my place again. I get caught up thinking about another part of the story until hours pass, and I have no more than one new paragraph written.

It didn't used to be this way for me. Before the car accident, I was never at a loss for words. I'm naturally inquisitive and during college, at Brigham Young University, I even liked to sit at the front of a class, so my professor would notice me right away. I always made a point to ask questions on the first day, just to hear the sound of my own voice. One time, my classmate in *Philosophy of Art* even begged me to stop asking questions so we could move forward in the textbook.

I don't like hearing the sound of my own voice anymore. I constantly lose my train of thought, stumble, and forget basic words. I usually know what I'm trying to say, I just can't remember the expressions, so I speak in circles, disguising my poor memory with filler words like *um, and, whatever, anyway.*

I have no memory of the accident. The only reason I even know it happened is because my family told me, and I vaguely remember the last few weeks in the hospital. My mom kept a journal, of which I've read every word multiple times, and she also took photographs of me. I'm taken aback when I see this stuff because, for a long time, I didn't understand how badly I was injured. Some of these photos are almost unrecognizable.

After I left the hospital, I expected my life to return to normal. I'd immediately go back to BYU, complete my degree, attend graduate school, find a great job, and live happily ever after. Unfortunately, life with a brain injury isn't so simple. Things that were once easy for me suddenly became difficult. I started articulating my frustrations in a journal, which developed into this memoir, so now I have many of the details in one place. My writing is also an attempt to reveal what it's like to live with an injured brain.

Traumatic Brain Injury is often called the silent epidemic because it handicaps people in ways that are invisible. We appear normal and fine on the surface, not exhibiting obvious signs of an injury, as most of the damage is internal. Survivors have impaired cognitive abilities such as getting easily overloaded, difficulty staying focused, balance and coordination problems, a sleep disorder, and a terrible short-term memory. My memory has improved over time, but for the first nine years after the accident, I constantly carried around scrap pieces of paper with the words "note to self," followed by instructions of what I was supposed to do. I felt misplaced without these notes.

As a writer, I think my chapters are short and choppy. I've tried to be completely truthful about everything I can remember from the past 14 years, which isn't much, and my mom's journal entries are sometimes cryptic. In some places, I can only write what seems accurate; what makes sense for the sake of the story. That being said, my writing is choppy because my thoughts are choppy. This really bothered me for a long time, which is one reason it took me so long to finish. I'm okay with it now because finally I can appreciate how far I've come by completing my memoir. What first began as just a need to understand what happened to me has developed into a personal record of conquering a trial that I never expected to endure. But then again, a person doesn't know how much they can handle until they are faced with a challenge.

1

Note to Self: You Work at the United Way

One of the keys to happiness is a bad memory.

~Rita Mae Brown

"Good morning, Jennifer!" Bill said brightly as I walked into the United Way office building. He was the perky older man with a friendly, contagious smile, who sat across from me at my desk in the fundraising office.

"Hi Bill!" I think my voice sounded as bright as his. Smiling, I glanced down at my little section of the long work table, and gasped when I saw all the papers. I remembered organizing it the day before, but it looked like a jumbled mess to me.

What am I supposed to do today? What are my tasks? I specifically remember writing them down somewhere! My heart palpitated. My head throbbed. I knew I'd made a list! How could I forget so soon?

I fumbled through the papers until I uncovered a *Post It* note that said, "Call these accounts tomorrow." It was stuck to a list of companies that I was supposed to contact and help kick off their United Way fundraising campaign. The beating in my heart slowed and I relaxed. Just then my manager came in to ask Victor, another United Way employee, to follow him and get his picture taken for his security badge.

I hadn't had mine taken either, so I followed them to the makeshift photo studio in our building's basement. Three men squeezed their way upstairs, while we tried to make our way down. I was nervous. *People walking up. People walking down. Don't slip and kill yourself. Going to photo studio. Hold on to railing. Watch where you're going,* I told myself. There were so many things to think about at once.

"Hi Jennifer!" one of the men smiled at me. "See ya back upstairs in the office," he said, as he climbed the steps. I smiled, as if I knew him and what he was talking about, even though I had no idea. Victor hopped down the stairs, but I just pushed myself against the wall and waited until everyone passed.

When I finally made it to the studio, the photographer was surprised to see me. "Jennifer, didn't we take yours yesterday?" he asked. After looking around the studio, things did seem familiar. Feeling foolish, I admitted my memory lapse, but he took my photo again anyway, just to be sure.

After he finished, I returned to the improvised office where our entire United Way team sat on folding chairs next to long tables; it felt like a college classroom. I sat in my usual middle seat and sighed once I saw the mess of papers again. *Where do I start?*

"So, did you get your ID badge, Jennifer?" I looked up across the table to see the same man who almost bumped into me on the stairs.

"Oh, um, hi," I answered. "Yeah, I got the picture but they won't have the badges for a couple days." I guess I knew this guy after all since he sat near me. I couldn't remember his name, so I pretended I was too busy to talk.

After stacking my papers, I realized that I didn't have any more donation slips. I knew there were some extra on the little shelf at the other side of the room, so I quickly scribbled, "Get more donation slips," on a yellow *Post-it*, slapped it on my face so I wouldn't forget what I needed, and walked over to the shelf.

Victor stopped me along the way to ask a question, while Bill smiled and made a joke about the note on my face. "You're so funny!" he said, pointing to my cheek. At first I didn't know what he was talking about, but then I remembered the *Post–it*, and pulled it off my face. I smiled, turned towards the shelf and grabbed more slips. I hastily pushed my way back, feeling glad that no one talked to me along the short way. I didn't have a *Post-it* telling me to go back to my desk.

As soon as I sat in my seat, I forgot what I was doing again, so I searched my papers for help. "Call these accounts to launch campaign," I read. A note next to one account said that I'd already called once, but only left a message. I decided to contact them first, and ask the preliminary questions. I dialed the number and a woman answered.

"Hi, this is Jennifer from the United Way of Minneapolis Area. Are you going to be the campaign coordinator this year?"

"Yeah?" she answered, her voice inflection raised slightly to ask a question. "Haven't we talked about this before? Remember? We decided I'd create a raffle for those who donate to the United Way. You called me two days ago."

I had no memory of ever speaking to this woman. Apologetically, I thanked her and hung up. How could I forget I'd talked to her already? From the corner of my eye, I saw Bill scurrying towards me.

"C'mon Jennifer, it's time for the United Way Training. We're all supposed to be outside on the grassy area across the street."

"Oh, yes of course," I lied. I guess I just forgot. After Bill and I made our way outside, we sat in a large circle with the other fundraisers.

Did I remember to put on deodorant this morning? The intense Minnesota humidity immediately made me sweat. The sun glistened brightly, causing the damp blades of grass to shimmer. I looked down at the soggy grass beneath me and wondered if it felt like I did: wet and uncomfortable.

We listened to a professional trainer talk about how to motivate our corporate sponsors to donate money to the United Way. I gazed up, but the bright sun blocked my view. It didn't really matter because I was barely able to pay attention. I felt nauseated and my head spun.

This was my first official job after graduating from Brigham Young University. It didn't completely relate to my bachelor's degree in humanities, but I'd convinced myself that working for the United Way made me a professional humanitarian.

"Jennifer? Jennifer?" I heard someone calling my name. Still squinting, I looked up to find the trainer talking to me.

"Yes?" I answered, scanning the circle of people around me, searching for clues about what we we'd been discussing.

"Your company? You were loaned to the United Way from what company?" Bill quietly whispered in my ear.

"Oh, I'm not loaned from any company," I answered, explaining my status, while still holding my hand above my eyes, as I tried to block the blinding sun. "I was hired directly by the United Way."

The humidity was making me feel nauseous again. We'd been there for what seemed like hours, doing team building exercises and learning about the organization.

"The United Way system includes approximately 1,350 community-based United Way organizations. Each is independent, separately incorporated and governed by local volunteers," the speaker droned on and her words trailed off.

I wasn't even paying attention. I just sat and touched the damp grass. *It must have rained recently*, I thought. I loved the rain. Quietly, I giggled to myself as I remembered Stacie and me frantically running to Spanish class in the middle of a rainstorm during our college study abroad to Chile. We were supposed to give a presentation to our Chilean culture class, but we overslept during our siesta after lunch. That Chilean rainstorm was more than two years earlier, but it seemed like just yesterday.

And just think, you almost didn't go to Chile, I said to myself. A few years earlier, I had told my dad I wanted to study abroad for a semester, and I'd looked at programs in Israel, London, and Chile.

"Traveling is for after college, Jen," my dad told me. For some reason, he thought if I left Provo, Utah, I wouldn't return. This is probably because he dropped out of the University of Minnesota to play golf in Florida, and feared the same thing would happen to me. He didn't want me to leave, which only made me want to go more, so I got my own cash together and told him, "I'm going."

I rubbed my hand back and forth along the damp grass again, and wondered what my life would be like if I'd just remained in Chile for the rest of the summer, or returned to BYU with my brother, Brent, a week earlier than I did.

Why didn't my car have airbags? It was just an accident, but sometimes I wish I was the one driving along interstate 80 in Nebraska, and not Kyrra.

2

Note to Self: Get Airbags on Next Car

You don't choose your family. They are God's
gift to you, as you are to them.

~Desmond Tutu

Brent is eighteen months older than me, but sometimes we're mistaken for twins. We attended BYU at the same time, had the same college major and even sat next to each other during class. Of course, usually we made the 18 hour road trip together from Minnesota back to Utah at the end of every summer. But 1994 was different.

He left a day earlier than I did to attend a wedding. My 17-year-old friend, Kyrra, had a family reunion in Utah at the same time as school started, so she and I agreed to drive together. I remember standing outside my parents' house as my mom photographed us in front of my Mitsubishi Montero. The overstuffed car had everything I owned jammed into it, including my stereo and the original Luis Guzman painting I'd purchased a few months earlier in Chile at the bargain price of $150. I remember Kyrra practicing how to drive a manual transmission at a rest-stop somewhere in Nebraska, sometime before the accident. This is my last memory for several months.

My mom was at work when she received a call from a nurse who broke the news. "This is Shermaine Sterkel from Regional West Medical Center in Scottsbluff, Nebraska. I'm calling about your daughter. Are you sitting down, Mrs. Mosher?"

"Oh, no, no don't ask me that!" she answered, as that question is usually followed by bad news. Mom's heart nearly pounded through her chest.

"Your daughter was seriously injured in a car accident in Kimball, Nebraska. She's been transported to us in critical condition with two broken legs, a fractured neck, and a very serious head injury."

My mom became frantic and started cussing, which was out of character for her. She grabbed her purse, ready to make a run for the door. As soon as her co-workers found out what happened, they offered to drive her home.

"No, I need my car. I've gotta drive myself," she screamed, in hysterics. "Wait, no wait—first I have to call Tom," and she dialed my dad's work number. There was no answer, so she only left a message.

Mom drove home like a mad-woman, speedily weaving in and out of traffic. "I wasn't safe to be on the road," she later admitted. "But I didn't care. I had to get home. I needed to get a hold of Tom and Brent."

She didn't have Brent's new phone number yet, so Mom called my friend, Deiudon, and begged her to find him. Deiudon only knew approximately where he lived, so she drove around until she saw his car parked in a driveway.

Brent happened to be upstairs unpacking when she rang his doorbell. His roommate, Scott, answered the door. "Is Brent here?" she asked, in a distressed tone.

"Yeah, he's here," he answered, completely unaware of what had occurred. "Brent, come down here, you already have visitors!"

He ran to the front door, surprised to see Deiudon. "I found you by looking for your car," she said, her voice shaking. "Your sister has been in a car accident." She didn't know the extent of it, only that it was bad and he was supposed to call home.

Brent scurried next door to use his neighbor's phone, since his wasn't even hooked up yet and my dad answered. Apparently, Dad already received a call from the hospital at the same time that Mom recklessly drove herself home from work. They both made it to our house just minutes apart.

"Mom and I are flying to Nebraska in a few hours," Dad told him.

"Can I come? There's no reason for me to stay in Provo anymore, without Jennifer. I'll meet you guys there."

Scott drove Brent to the airport and they were both silent in the car, except for the moment when he told Scott, "I know I won't be back very soon." My mom later told me Brent knew before he even got to the airport that he'd drop out of school for the year, or for as long as I needed him.

When they arrived at the Salt Lake City International Airport, he called home again to tell our parents he'd gotten his ticket at half-price for bereavement. Not that a discounted airline ticket was any consolation, but it seems worth noting as this was the first in a series of gifts that our family received.

Brent made it to the hospital 30 minutes before my parents. As soon as Mom and Dad walked in, the receptionist went back to get a nurse who would take them into my room. As they waited, another receptionist paged a physician to explain my condition. This physician was Dr. Tom White, the surgeon assigned to my care.

My injuries were life-threatening and I needed medical attention fast. Regional West Medical Center was the closest level II Trauma Center to Kimball; located 40 miles away in Scottsbluff, a town of just under 15,000 people. This was very small compared to our home in Minneapolis with a population of over 375,000. Dad even describes the hospital as having a "small-town, everybody knows your name feeling to it." I received wonderful, personalized care there. My favorite parts of Mom's journal are all the places she writes about the relationship she developed with the staff at Regional West.

"Your nurse, Duane," she wrote, "once told me to put clunky, oversized high-top tennis shoes on your feet, so you wouldn't get foot drop from laying comatose for so long (a deficit that develops when your toes and ankles turn upwards; you drag the front of your foot on the ground when you walk)." She still keeps these shoes in her cedar chest at home. "I don't know why I kept them. I guess just as a reminder of how far Jennifer has come." The shoes must have worked because I don't have foot drop now, and my gait is normal.

"In addition to changing your IV and giving you medication, Duane treated you like a real person," Brent told me. "He was always making sure you looked comfortable." Once, he said, Duane let him help lift me from the bed to a gurney while they changed my bed sheets. "That stuff meant a lot to me. He always kept us involved."

Even today, Mom, Dad and Brent talk about my doctors and nurses at Regional West as if they're family. I've heard countless other stories of people who hate the hospital where their loved ones are being treated; feeling like nothing more than a number to unattached doctors. Our experience wasn't like this in Nebraska. I was in the ICU longer than any other patient at the time, so the entire department knew everything about my care. Brent later said, "It seemed like someone (the hospital staff) was always in your room, just checking on you. They took great pride in your recovery."

Brent told me what it was like the first time they saw me after the accident. He said you enter the intensive care unit through two sets of double doors. The first are large oak doors, the second are metal automatic doors. My room was the first one on the left. They walked in, stunned by what they saw. I lay motionless, and my entire body was thick. My hands and eyes were bloated, and my head was shaven on one side. There was a long, stitched cut from the top left corner of my forehead all the way back to the middle of my head. I had tubes in my mouth, connecting to a ventilator that controlled my breathing. My legs hung in traction, suspended by white, canvas straps and pins ran through my tibia bones, connecting to cords from which hung heavy weights that were used to pull the broken bones back into position.

"I'm sorry about the horrible car accident," Dr. White said, when he walked into my room to greet my family. "We're doing everything we can to help Jennifer." He continued explaining the specifics of my injury, but after describing the contraptions holding my broken legs together, my dad fainted and fell forward towards my bed. Luckily, Brent was able to catch him before he fell on top of me. From then on, the doctors asked my dad to remain seated when he came into my room.

The initial medical assessment did not look promising. Dr. White wrote the following evaluation:

> *This young lady is badly injured. She has multiple traumatic injuries with a severe head injury, and a Glasgow Coma score of 3 to 4[1]. There is no obvious operable lesion on the CAT scan, but she is paralyzed and sedated to keep her intracranial pressures controlled. The only movement I saw before paralysis was a purposeless left arm movement. She has a C-1, C-2 fracture and bilateral mid-shaft femur fractures. She will be started on antibiotics, admitted to the Intensive Care Unit and given Tetanus Prophylaxis.*

My family soon learned the accident details from the hospital staff, which in turn, had learned them from the police.

---

[1] The Glascow Coma Scale is scored between three and fifteen. Three is the worst possible score and fifteen is the best. Dr. White later told me that even a corpse is given a score of three on this scale.

They think I rested my legs on the dashboard as Kyrra drove along Interstate 80 in Kimball. A gust of wind might have hit the SUV because within seconds the car tumbled and rolled five times into the median. My legs stuck out the passenger-side window, and a deep laceration sliced across my forehead, peeling my scalp from front to back. Kyrra sprained her wrist in the rollover, and I was unconscious.

There happened to be a fireman and a physician's assistant driving behind our car; they both stopped to help. One of the men found a piece of plywood, and he manually put my legs in traction while the other held my neck straight. They told the state trooper who arrived on the scene, "She's bad. I don't think she'll make it to the hospital."

An ambulance took us both to the local hospital where they were able to stabilize me until an Airforce Emergency Transport from Cheyenne, Wyoming brought me to Regional West Medical Center. This rapid flight only took seventeen minutes. The pilot was so concerned about my injuries that he called the hospital twice to check on my condition after he left.

Brent, Mom, and Dad all slept in the hospital that first night. My parents squished side-by-side on a reclining chair in my room, and Brent slept on two footstools pushed together. The next morning, worn out, they walked to the hotel across the street to get a room. They had just arrived when Mom got a call from Dr. Ernie Beehler, my neurosurgeon who said, "Do you know how seriously your daughter is hurt?" He explained that I might not make it through the night.

My exhausted mother surprised herself by screaming at the doctor, "Don't you dare tell me that over the phone! We'll be right there." They ran over to the hospital to talk with Dr. Beehler face to face. Standing at a nurses' desk, right outside my room, he let them know about the swelling in my brain.

"The CT scan did not reveal any architecture on her brain. Our brain looks a lot like cauliflower, with ridges and valleys, and this structure has been swollen away," Dr. Beehler explained. "I can't tell you what her injuries mean, or what disabilities they will cause, but the increasing pressure building up in her skull could soon cause her death, or she could never wake up at all. We need to see some sort of movement from her, to know that she's still in there."

My family lost it after this conversation. They went into my room, and sobbed uncontrollably for more than ten minutes. The rest of the day was dismal, just sitting around, waiting for updates, waiting to see, as Dr. Beehler had said, some sort of movement from me.

That night, something remarkable happened. They were back in my room; it was dark, probably ten o'clock. The lights were off, except for one small light by the door. Dad clasped my hand, and quietly whispered, "Sweet Jennifer..." just before he saw me slightly look towards him, and softly squeeze his hand.

"Brent! Loretta! Jennifer moved!" my dad screamed. Mom repeated my name, and cried tears of joy. Brent broke down and sobbed so hard he had to leave the room. This was a defining moment because, as Brent later told me, I was "always one step ahead of Dr. Beehler." If he said, "We need to see her do this...," then I would do it. Each small step showed them I was very slowly on the path to recovery.

Finally, they met with the neurologist, Dr. Terry Himes, who let them know that at least I'd live. "She might never be the same person," he explained. "She might have difficulty speaking, she may have a different personality, and she probably won't return to college." He spent an entire hour and a half talking with them, and all of his words were difficult to hear. All except for one statement that everyone clung to when they needed hope. He said, "Jennifer will still have the same spirit and you will still love her." His advice continued, "Regardless of how much she recovers, she won't remember much about her time in the hospital, so I recommend you keep a journal for her."

My mom diligently wrote in her own journal every night anyway, so she immediately started one for me. On Sunday, August 28th, five days after the accident, she wrote:

Jennifer looks like a beat-up old lady, and has been lying silently in her hospital bed for days now. There is a large, thick collar around her neck. Although her bulging eyes sometimes look half open, there is no movement from her today. She looks like she is in a peaceful, deep sleep. Dr. Himes told us the most damage was done to the left side of her brain which controls the language and speech. She'll probably have some disabilities relating to this. Her nurse today is named Kathleen. She is wonderful and explains everything she does.

"I don't tell people this very often," she said, "but I have seen two other miracles leave this room and I really feel like Jennifer will be the third."

My parents and Brent developed a regular routine in Nebraska. Every Monday, Dad drove himself to the airport to catch a flight from Scottsbluff to Denver, and then from Denver to Minneapolis where he tried to keep his construction company together; he returned to Scottsbluff every weekend. Each weekday, Brent and my mom took turns waiting in my hospital room, hoping to witness an eye blink or a hand lift. Sundays they went together to The Church of Jesus Christ of Latter-day Saints, where many people were willing to help. A different member of the church had them over for dinner almost every night. My family says they gained a deeper understanding of service during this time because never before have they felt so helpless, and had such a "need" to be served.

A few days into my recovery, Mom, Dad, and Brent got to the hospital early in the morning, and a nurse was already in my room. "Jennifer is not doing so well," she told them. "Her sodium count has dropped, and she's not responding to the medication. Dr. Himes has already been in, but left to order another CT scan for her." Mom gasped, while Dad and Brent plopped down on separate chairs and buried their faces in their hands. Just then, Dr. Himes returned with the test results.

"I have good news," he announced. "I didn't see any changes on her scan, so I think the unresponsiveness is due to the medication we've used. I'm cutting back some on the Phenobarbital (an anti-seizure medication) and on the morphine (a painkiller), which could be making her more drowsy."

For the rest of the day, my family just sat in my room waiting and hoping to see any sort of reaction from me. The next week was the same. *Waiting and hoping. Waiting and hoping.*

I feel as if now I'm telling a story about someone other than myself: *this happened,* and then *that happened*; a documentary of quick takes about a person, who also happens to be me. I'm not writing from memory, nor am I embellishing my injuries. I was there, but I wasn't. This is about my life, but it's not. It's surreal. These are details that my mom recorded in her journal, and I'm just recounting them, second hand.

Wednesday, August 31, 1994, was a pivotal day for everyone. It was just eight days after the accident, and Mom and Brent arrived at the hospital before 6:30 A.M. (Dad returned home to work for the rest of the week), and sat next to my bed for a while, until Dr. Himes walked in to examine me. He turned to my mom and said, "Loretta, I'm going to go ahead and do another MRI, so we can see how her organs and tissues are progressing."

"Okay," she flatly agreed. "That's fine. I'm just going to walk down the hall for a minute to stretch my legs. I'll be back." Brent followed her.

They left the room and didn't get more than halfway down the hallway when they heard Dr. Himes yelling, "Hey, Mom you better come here! I got a response!"

My mom and Brent bolted back into my room, expecting to watch me sit up, smile, and ask, "Where am I?" But everything looked the same as it had a few moments earlier. Dr. Himes was still standing next to my bed, and I still lay practically motionless.

"I think I got a small response from her," Dr. Himes explained. "It's not much, but I asked Jennifer to look at me, and she turned her head towards my voice. She seems to be more alert if you talk to her." He left the room to order an MRI.

Mom's lips quivered, as a tear streamed down her cheek. "Jennifer, I'll do anything for you. I'll turn cartwheels, anything, just please keep getting better," she pleaded, rubbing her hand softly against my arm. "If you want me to keep massaging your arm, just squeeze my hand." My mom said I gave her hand a big squeeze. "Brent! Did you see that? She squeezed my hand!"

This moment was the second in a very gradual series of instances as I emerged from a coma that lasted almost four weeks. Mom later describes it like "watching a baby being born." She'd see just a little response, such as a gentle head turn, a hand squeeze, or a slight curve in the corner of my lips, almost a smile. As each day went on, I looked brighter and more alert than I had the day before. But, I still wasn't speaking. I wasn't walking, and I wasn't eating. I wasn't doing any of the normal, unassisted life skills that an adult is supposed to be able to do. Like Mom said, I was almost a newborn again, and no one had any idea how much more I would grow.

I'm indebted to my mom for diligently recording details in her journal, especially now as I try to piece together information and understand what happened to me. I've spent so much time wondering how I was going to function with a brain injury that I never really thought about what it was like for my terrified parents to watch their injured daughter in the hospital. Her journal is a glimpse of the unconditional love that parents feel for their children.

Mom tried to be positive, but that wasn't always possible. "I have my really bad moments," she wrote. "When I think about what *could* happen, that Jennifer *could* die, or she *could* be spastic, then I feel depressed. If Jennifer hurts, our family hurts. But, I also know if I don't take care of myself, then I won't be much help to them. I need to pull it together. So, I'm not going to let any negative thought come into my mind," she decided. It was the night after making this decision that Mom had a dream that strengthened her capacity to cope. Again, she wrote about this in her journal:

> *Finally, I've been able to sleep. For two nights in a row, I dreamt about Jennifer at different stages during her recovery: in a wheelchair, learning to walk again, and with a Halo Brace[2] on her head. Then the next morning, I combed my hair while looking in the mirror, and another thought flashed through my mind: Brent and Jennifer graduating college together. I take these as messages from God and they bring me hope.*

From then on, she felt stronger every day. "I just have to believe that Jennifer is going to be okay," Mom told herself. This deliberate positive thinking helped her start smiling a little, and her sense of humor even returned.

Eighteen days after the accident, she called the hospital early in the morning to see how I was doing. My nurse, Kelly, answered the phone. "Everything is stable, Loretta, except Jennifer bumped the button on her bed, and raised her head way up. So, I unhooked the motor just in case," she explained.

"Oh! That must've looked pretty funny to watch the bed go up and down," my mom quietly whispered into the phone, and they both started giggling.

"Why are you whispering?" Kelly asked.

"Well, because I don't want to wake up Tom. He's still sleeping," Mom answered softly.

"What Loretta?" my dad yelled from the bed. "What? I can't hear you!" He must have heard my mom say his name and assumed she was talking to him. Neither of my parents slept very deeply during this time.

---

[2] A Halo Brace is a metal ring secured to the skull with pins and to two metal rods attached to a well-fitted plastic jacket securing complete immobility of the cervical spine.

"I'm not talking to you!" my mom answered back, almost in banter, but still in a whisper.

Kelly heard this short conversation and laughed over the phone. "You guys are pretty funny."

"We've got to laugh about anything we can these days, to keep our sanity," Mom responded.

On Thursday, September 15, 1994, 23 days after the accident, Mom wrote in her journal: "I didn't sleep well last night because I was so worried about Jennifer." She called the hospital and talked to another nurse named Kathy.

"Jennifer has been pretty ornery this morning," she explained. "She pulls off her heart monitor, I put it back on and she pulls it off again. It's like she's playing a little game with me." Mom got really excited because if the nurse recognized that I was playing games, it meant my personality was returning. Later that afternoon, she got even more excited.

Brent and my mom sat in the hospital room, exercising my arms. "You're doing great, Jennifer," Mom cheered. "You're really progressing and I'm so proud of you." And then she asked me for a hug. I reached up my arms and pulled my mom towards my chest to give her a genuine, sincere, half-hug. She said it was the sweetest hug she'd ever received. Clearly I was responding to her.

"Can your brother have one too?" Brent asked, and I pulled him down towards me, to give the same gentle hug, and they both started applauding; not that I could hear them, but it was another sign that I was coming around.

Just then, my anesthesiologist stopped in my room, to get an update on my condition, as all of my doctors often did. "Hi! What's all the excitement about?" he wondered.

"Jennifer just hugged us both!" Mom was elated, as if I was a toddler who had just taken her first steps.

"That's great news! I stopped in earlier this morning, and noticed that Jennifer *is* looking brighter." He sounded just as thrilled. "I'll post signs around the hospital."

"That's what's so great about this place," Mom wrote. "Everyone knows Jennifer, and is concerned about her. I know we'd never find this same kind of intimacy at a big-city hospital."

We spent just over four weeks in Nebraska, all of which time I have no memory. According to the hospital discharge report, I was able to let ice chips thaw inside my mouth, and I had begun taking minimal sips of water. On September 28, 1994, I was stable enough for Mom and I to board a two-engine air ambulance bound for a hospital in Minneapolis. Mom wrote in her journal that some of my nurses, Duane, Kathy, and Kelly, cried when we said good-bye to them.

Two pilots and two flight medics accompanied us on our flight home. Strapped to a cot, I was so agitated that I flung my arms from side-to-side until the medics gave me a sedative so I'd relax. The drug didn't work for very long. Each time they tried to clip an oxygen tube near my nose, I'd frantically pull it away. Finally, they just held it close, but whenever I felt too much air blowing at me, I'd pull the towel over my face.

As the plane got closer to the airport in Minneapolis, the urban lights sparkled and my mom felt the city's energy. "Finally we're coming home," she said to herself. "Five weeks is a long time to be away, especially in a small town like Scottsbluff, Nebraska, under such miserable circumstances." When we landed, an ambulance was waiting to deliver us to Abbott Northwestern Hospital, which would be my home for one week until I could be admitted into Sister Kenny Rehabilitation Institute.

3

Note to Self: Go to Therapy

A hospital is no place to be sick.

~Samuel Goldwyn

Three days into my stay at Abbott Northwestern Hospital, four nurses came into my room and asked my family to step out. This wasn't unusual. Hospital staff often came to administer some drug or to perform a medical procedure, and typically they asked any visitors to leave.

Brent and my mom left to wait in a small, nearby area until they heard a sad moaning and occasional powerful yelping coming from my room. Brent sprang up from his chair and tossed the magazine he was looking through onto the floor.

"Mom! Do you hear that? It's Jennifer; you better go check on her!"

Mom scurried off, shoved my hospital room door open to see me lying on my back with two female nurses holding me down, and two male nurses prying my legs apart as I squealed in fear.

"What the hell are you doing?!" Mom screamed.

"Mrs. Mosher, she has a yeast infection, and we're having trouble getting the suppository inside of her."

"Get away from her! She probably thinks she's being raped," Mom shouted and they quickly pulled away. "Just because she's brain-injured doesn't mean she doesn't get scared or feel pain!"

My mom protested to the hospital administration and received a direct apology from the department head. She was told that if I had the same problem again, I'd be given a pill by mouth to cure a yeast infection. The entire floor in the hospital heard about the incident, and one of the male nurses involved even gave my mom a letter of apology. Mom wrote about this experience in her journal.

"This is the reason I need to be with Jennifer at all times in the hospital. She can't defend herself, and I know her better than they do," she recorded.

A bigger hospital in Minneapolis meant more options, but it also meant thicker red-tape. Our insurance company approved a seven-day evaluation period at Sister Kenny, and I could stay only if I made continual improvement. If not, I'd be sent to a nursing home. "Over my dead body!" Mom declared. "My daughter is not going to a nursing home!" Luckily, this didn't happen because eventually I was officially admitted into the program.

As I said before, I don't remember anything about my month at Regional West Medical Center, and it wasn't until a couple weeks at Sister Kenny that the details of my therapy sessions began to stick.

I do know that my mom always pushed me eagerly down the hospital corridor to therapy, not stopping for anyone along the way. It didn't matter who brought me, but they always did it with gusto, as if the faster I got there, the faster I'd recover. We even rolled past my doctor at times, and usually Mom would jump at the chance to talk with him, since he only checked in on me occasionally. Once she asked him, "How do you think Jennifer is doing?"

"*What you see is what you get,*" he answered.

"I see progress!" she proclaimed.

The truth is he didn't know what would become of me. No one did. Many patients injured as severely as I was didn't survive, let alone recover.

Mom wrote that as soon as we rolled into occupational therapy one day, I turned to Joette, my therapist, and asked her, "How'd you like to live in this chair?" It was the first thing I'd said all morning. But at least I was speaking. It wasn't until September 23rd, still in Nebraska one month after the accident, that I even mumbled my first words. The only reason I know this is because my mom wrote about it in her journal:

> *Brent got Jennifer to say "hello" today! I was out running errands, and when I got back to the hospital room, Brent said, "Say hello to Mom, Jennifer."*
>
> *In a very low, very raspy voice, she said "Hello Mom, hello Mom." They were the most beautiful words I'd ever heard. I've waited so long for this. Then Jennifer puckered up and gave me kisses. I think she was excited to finally be able to express herself.*
>
> *"Welcome back, Jennifer!" I said. I've waited so long for this moment.*

When we finally arrived to the occupational therapy room, Mom waited off to the side while Joette set several small, wooden pieces on the table. "Jennifer," she said. "Let's put this puzzle together."

"Uuuh." Pause. "Uuuh." Pause. "Uuuh." Over and over, I could hear a grunting from across the therapy room. I watched an older man hunch over his walker, while two women dressed in scrubs stood next to him, gently massaging his back to quiet him. The man kept grunting and blankly staring off into space. I wished he'd stop making that unbearable, irritating noise.

On the other side of the room, another man slowly passed a large, blue rubber ball to a nurse and she passed it back to him. Only Joette and I sat at the therapy table, so I stopped looking at everyone else and stared down at the puzzle.

Joette turned it over, dumping four pieces onto the table. "Jennifer, can you put these back in the right places for me?" She asked it in the same gentle, high-pitched tone someone would use while talking to a child.

It didn't feel condescending, though. I liked being around Joette. She was positive, but not perky in an annoying, patronizing way like some of the other therapists. Joette loved her job, or at least I felt like she loved her job, which made me want to do well. Plus, I got the impression that she liked working with me. Whenever I felt like someone at the hospital was put out by having to take care of me, I didn't try to improve.

"Oh–oh, ouch," a cardboard piece jabbed my palm, while my head throbbed. I dropped my forehead into my hands because I couldn't figure out how to assemble the puzzle. Not only did I ache inside, but I was mortified as I looked around the room. Most other patients were elderly, as if an ailment had already taken control of their bodies. *Why was I in this strange place? Who are these odd people?*

Joette caught on to my confusion, and again explained, "Jennifer, put each puzzle piece back into its place." I watched her put one puzzle piece back into the cardboard base.

I tried to copy her and held a piece in my hand. I waited. And I waited. *What do I do now?* I waited for my brain to send a signal to my hand. *Where do I put the piece?* The answer should have been obvious, as this was an activity suitable for a small child. But, the signal never came, so I decided to just put my piece next to Joette's. This battle between my brain and my hand went on for more than 20 minutes before I finally had all four pieces in the correct place.

"Jennifer, it's time for your nap," a nurse interrupted our session. It felt like I'd been working on the puzzle forever, anyway, so I was glad to be done. But, I was hardly interested in going back to my room to sleep. In my injured brain, I thought everyone was always bossing me around, forcing me to do things I didn't want to do.

"I'm not even tired!" I tried to scream with all the zeal I could muster, but really I spoke softly. I raised my right hand up to hit the nurse, and she blocked my weak arm before I could reach her. Mom tells me I hit people at the hospital, which was unexpected at first because I'd always been calm and good-natured. I rarely even yelled at people. We now understand that most Traumatic Brain Injury survivors experience a frantic stage of confusion and agitation on their path to recovery.

"Jennifer! Stop; just relax. I think you need a break from therapy," the nurse said.

While she helped me into the wheelchair, Joette smiled, touched my shoulder, and said, "Great work today, Jennifer. You're working really hard. I'm proud of you."

I felt good inside after she said this because it was true. Hard work was one of the few things I still remembered how to do. Since I liked Joette, and since she was so nice to me, I wanted to please her. Maybe she'd realize that I wasn't at all where I was supposed to be, and finally someone would save me.

The nurse pushed me back to my room where I lay down on the bed. I tried to roll my head to the left or right, but my metal Halo Brace blocked the turns. So, I just moved my eyes from side-to-side, with a perplexed look, as I mulled over my condition.

Naps are nothing but wasted time, I told myself. *First they make me assemble a puzzle suitable for a kid, now I'm forced to take a nap when I don't even feel tired, and to top it all off, I'm locked up in this stupid place. How am I going to get out of here? I'll never see my family again!* I started concocting an escape plan, but these thoughts consumed me for only a few minutes until I drifted off to sleep.

"Jennifer, sweetheart—wake up, I'm here and you told me to wake you up," I could hear my mom's voice. I don't remember saying anything to her about waking me up, or how long I'd been sleeping, but I was happy to finally see her.

"Mom, you make me feel so good. I don't see you very often," we embraced as my Halo Brace brushed her earlobe.

"Honey, I see you every day, but you don't remember." I didn't understand why she was tricking me because it didn't feel like I'd seen her recently. "I was here this morning for your therapy," she explained.

"Hmmm!" I said sharply, almost like a question, "Why didn't you wake up me up right when you got here?"

"I did wake you up. I even gave you a hug!"

I still couldn't remember seeing my mom in the morning, but I guess I had no reason not to trust her. "Well, tomorrow morning when you come, make sure you wake me real hard."

"I'll wake you as hard as I can," she promised.

Each morning was like the beginning of a new life because I didn't remember what I'd accomplished the day before. Not only did an occupational therapist need to help me assemble an easy puzzle, but a nurse had to help me in and out of my wheelchair because I couldn't walk.

Several weeks into my recovery, a physical therapist put me in front of two parallel bars, nodded and said, "Jennifer, I'm here to help, but I challenge you to give walking a try." Mom watched as I tried walking between the bars. At first, my steps were unsteady, but I kept trying. Before long I was slowly moving up and down the hospital corridors with a walker.

One morning, Gary, a kind, retired physical therapist who came up to the hospital once per week as a volunteer, played the game *Follow the Leader* with me. He led the way as I trailed him around in my walker, through the hallways. "Follow me to the physical therapy room," he said.

"Okay, then open the door for me, Gary," I commanded. Again, my mom stood off to the side, watching as we played. She told me I had a grin on my face the entire time. In retrospect, I think it felt good to me because finally I was in control again. For so long at the hospital, I had to let others do everything for me. I couldn't feed myself, or walk, or use the toilet, or completely process ideas on my own, and this wasn't my style. At least it didn't used to be my style. I often wondered if the old me was waiting off to the side, pointing and laughing as if this was all a big joke.

Brent was the first person I saw when I woke up the next morning. I knew who he was, but I didn't know why I was in the hospital. "Why am I here? I don't understand why my body is so messed up," I asked. My entire body felt thick and hard as a rock, yet everyone told me I was thin and frail. The world looked strange and jumbled because I saw double of everything. While I waited for him to answer my question, I wondered why I had two poles nailed into my head, so I pulled it as hard as I could, trying to free myself from the contraption.

"Jennifer stop pulling at your Halo Brace! You were in a car accident on your way to college at BYU," Brent told me. "That's why you are in the hospital. You fractured your neck and both femurs." My eyes widened, surprised not because I'd been in a car accident, but because of something else he said.

"I'm in college?"

Looking around the white hospital room, I noticed some photographs plastered on the wall. "Who are those people?" I asked, while keeping one eye closed to veil my double vision.

There were three sharp looking young adults with me in this photo—two men and one woman. I could only see the woman's head as she was covered by the red flannel shirts both men wore. All of us were snuggled up to each other tightly, as if we tried to keep warm.

"Those are your friends from your college study abroad program in Chile," Brent said, pointing to a photo. "That's Ian and Sarah and Jory," he explained. "You told me all about them when you returned in April. You said you guys were always together."

I reached at my forehead as an attempt to ease my throbbing headache. But, before my fingers reached their destination, they were interrupted by a metal circle. Only seconds had passed since Brent ordered me to stop pulling on my brace, but he had to do it again because I pulled at it as hard as I could.

"Jennifer! Stop pulling at your Halo Brace! You were in a car accident on your way to BYU, after studying in Chile, and you fractured your neck and both femurs. You have a Traumatic Brain Injury," my brother patiently explained, again. "You need the brace on your head to heal your fractured neck."

Confused, I stopped pulling and asked a simple question, "Brent, when was I in Chile?"

"Seven months ago, Jennifer, with BYU Study Abroad for Winter Semester. Right now it's November 1994, you were injured almost three months ago in a car accident on your way back to school, after summer vacation," he explained again.

I said nothing. At least I didn't hear myself say anything out loud, but I'm not sure because a voice inside my head said, *I'm in college? It's bad that I'm in the hospital. Chile? I need to escape this place.*

"Jennifer! Time to get started!" A physical therapist walked into my room. "Brent, you can come too, if you'd like. We're going to the physical therapy room." Brent helped me sit up, while the therapist brought me my wheelchair. I hated how some therapists always had such high spirits getting me out of bed to do things I didn't want to do in the first place. Besides, I hurt all over, and nothing feels right when you're in physical pain.

They escorted me into a room filled with stationary bikes, treadmills, wooden stairs, and large rubber balls. I exercised regularly at the gym before my accident, so this room felt familiar. Once I got onto a bike, the weight of my Halo Brace had me leaning so far forward that I could barely pedal. I was like a small child riding a bicycle without training wheels for the first time. I had trouble balancing my feet, and it took all the energy I could muster to complete even one circle. *Why won't my legs work correctly?* I must have pedaled just three times around before feeling too exhausted to work anymore.

"Great job," I remember Brent saying, as I tried to pedal. "I'm so proud of my favorite sister!"

"I'm your *only* sister!"

We laugh about this now, but at the time, I didn't understand the sarcasm behind his claim, and couldn't get it out of my head as to why he'd say I was his favorite when neither of us had any other siblings. Brent still calls me his favorite sister. I still remind him that I'm his only sister.

A few days later, I concocted another escape plan. I didn't say anything out loud because my mom sat next to me. *I must have been kidnapped. Why else would I be here? The doctors are so cruel. One of them even drilled something metal into my skull. No one believes me; not Brent, not my parents. No one.* I pictured my life, locked up in the hospital forever. *Mom and Dad are clueless. Why can't they see it? They come up here every day, but never take me with them when they leave.* I didn't get it. I was doomed and needed help.

Lying on the bed, my mom watched me cup my hand over my ear as if I were talking on the phone. I clearly said, "This is Jennifer Mosher. Will you bring something up so I can cut this damn thing off my head!?" I don't know who I thought I'd talked to, and no one came to help me.

I asked Mom to call Taia. She didn't know why I wanted to call, but she was excited when I recalled anyone from my past. Taia had moved to Minneapolis from New York City, and we met at church. Although she was ten years older than me, we became instant friends. She was an artist and I loved art. She dressed in a creative, yet classy style, designing, and sewing her own clothes, and I loved fashion. She understood the flavorful difference between Pure Olive Oil and Extra Virgin Olive Oil (which we loved to discuss); she was a fabulous chef, so I loved eating anything she prepared.

When my mom passed me the phone receiver, I don't think she expected me to say what I said. "Oh Taia! Help me! I've been kidnapped. I'm in the hospital at Sitter Kenee Intooot (I always had trouble saying the full hospital name properly), and

I've got to get out of here! I was in a car accident. Did you know?" Of course Taia knew exactly where I was. I even had a photo of her sitting by my wheelchair one day in the hospital corridor.

The next day was the same as always: the nurse woke me up, dressed me, and I ate breakfast in the cafeteria. Earlier in my recovery, I was immobile and fed via a feeding tube in my stomach; eventually I was able to swallow food and sit up in a chair. But everything tasted disgusting, and I'd lost my appetite due to my medication, so I didn't eat much anyway. I'd lost more than twenty-five pounds.

Just like every night, my mom came to the hospital after work and stayed with me in my room until I fell asleep. I wondered if she would finally wise up and save me from the kidnappers. Once she lay with me on my bed as I tried to cuddle, but my Halo Brace smacked her in the nose.

"How many more days until I get this thing off?" I grabbed the brace, and pulled as hard as I could. "Why don't you help me mom?" I asked another question before she could even answer, "Why doesn't anyone ever come to visit me?"

"Oh, I think you forgot that last night your friends Steve and Nick came to visit you, and before that your cousins Richie and Brandie were here." I knew these people, but I couldn't remember them visiting me in the hospital.

Just then the phone rang, which wasn't unusual since we had many friends from our church and family in Minnesota. People always called my room, to ask if we needed anything, and to find out when they could come to visit. That time it was a friend from our church, and I'm told I'd seen him just a few months earlier at my birthday party, although I had no memory of this. As soon as I heard his voice, I somehow imagined I was talking to my boyfriend (I didn't even have a boyfriend then, and I barely knew this guy).

"Do you still love me?" I asked. "I've been kidnapped at the hospital!" I elbowed my mom after hearing her giggle.

That night the doctors decided to reduce my intake of Ativan, so I wouldn't hallucinate so much. Maybe this would help control my panic attacks about being kidnapped.

I remember making pizza with Joette, during occupational therapy a few days later. She set a box of flour, spices, and a can of sauce, pepperoni, and grated cheese on the counter. I was disappointed with the high-fat pepperoni, so I asked if I could make it with half just cheese. I searched for a large bowl to mix the dough, and tried to open the bags of flour and spices, but I didn't have enough strength do it, so Joette helped. I mixed the ingredients until the white flour was speckled with oregano flakes, basil, and garlic. I set the pizza pan on the counter while laughing and chit-chatting. For the first time since my injury, I felt like my old self, almost normal, like I was ready to leave the hospital. After looking at my mixture, and seeing that it didn't look like dough, I turned to Joette with a puzzled expression. *What do I do next? What is missing?*

"Don't worry Jennifer," Joette assured me. "We still need a little water to make the dough." She handed me a measuring cup filled with water, and I poured it into the bowl.

Once I finished mixing and rolling, I assembled the pizza and Joette set the oven to 350 degrees. Twenty minutes later I had the best-tasting homemade pizza I'd ever eaten. Who would've thought that baking pizza could be so rewarding and therapeutic?

4

Note to Self: You're Out of the Hospital

Our strength grows out of our weaknesses.

~Ralph Waldo Emerson

I will always remember Wednesday, November 23, 1994 because after 90 days, I was officially discharged from the hospital. It was especially momentous as this day was followed by the American Thanksgiving Holiday; a day to express gratitude.

Something important had to happen before I could leave the hospital. They needed to remove the metal Halo Brace attached to my skull for 78 days. At 7:50 A.M., a nurse came into my room to alert us that a doctor was on his way to liberate me. Soon we heard a knock at the door, and in walked Dr. John Mullan, a neurosurgeon for Sister Kenny Institute. The doctor calmly sat himself next to me, and reached for my head with what looked like pliers. *Grrr. Crackle. Screech.* I heard some awful noises, but soon I was free. My head felt so weak and weightless that, for a moment, I doubted it was still attached to my neck.

An hour later, Brent and my mom checked me out of the hospital, and I distinctly remember feeling an unusual freedom as I walked away. I was like a felon escaping from jail. Finally, I could feel my hair blowing in the wind. I could smell clean fresh air, and not the perpetual smell of gauze and Band-Aids; the inescapable smell of injury. I did have a cane in one hand, and held on to Brent's elbow with the other, but I was free.

"Here Jennifer, let me hold that," Mom said, taking my cane, carefully guiding me into the front seat. Brent was the designated driver, while Mom sat in the backseat. As we drove down our street in Minneapolis, I could see our home from a distance.

The small stucco house was a textbook reminder of my past, like looking through my high school yearbook. I could remember my prom date, Steve, ringing our front doorbell, my friend, Corinne, coming over to chat, and Brent marching in the front door after hockey practice with a smelly, oversized duffle bag flung over his shoulder, his face still dripping with sweat. These memories were short-lived, though, because after being at home for one full day, I realized that life in the real world would require an adjustment.

In the hospital, I focused solely on my recovery. People constantly told me it was a miracle I'd survived such a terrible accident, and that my diligent effort during therapy would speed up the recovery. There was specific, organized work for me to do. A nurse came at 8:30 A.M. to help me dress. Meals were delivered to my room three times per day. I even had a scheduled nap (regardless if I thought I needed one or not). A different therapist promptly came to pick me up for physical, occupational, and speech therapy. I always understood what I needed to do to succeed, and I was determined to make it happen.

Without the hospital, I had the arduous task of controlling my own recovery and coming to terms with my injury. Every night there were friends and family at our house, coming to see me. Maybe only a few people came, but in my injured brain it felt like an overwhelming daily 24 hours of non-stop visitors. During my first few weeks at home, I wondered how I was supposed to function. I wanted so badly to rest, but each time I lay in my bed to nap, nothing happened, as if I'd forgotten how to fall asleep.

Almost one month after my discharge, I was back at the hospital for testing from my speech therapist, Colleen, to evaluate my strengths and weaknesses. I scored the highest in spelling, but my auditory comprehension was just below the cut off, which meant I needed to rehearse some basic listening skills. Colleen asked me, "Which two words make up the conjunction 'I'll?'" I couldn't answer her. Just a few months earlier, I was two semesters away from a bachelor's degree in humanities-English, and now I'd tested with the reading skills of an elementary school student.

I didn't want to talk about my difficulty with anyone. My mom tried hard to get me to reveal that I carried some sort of shame about my injury. That's her favorite word: *shame*. She frequently told me and my brother about the dysfunctional home she grew up in, and how her own mother constantly shamed her. She avoided making her children feel inferior at all costs. Any indication that we felt any degree of shame about anything was my mother's greatest fear.

Shame is a painful feeling about oneself as a person, and I didn't feel exactly this way. I liked me, but I felt embarrassed about my injury. I hated my bad memory. I hated that I was slower, and I hated my slurred speech. Mom worried. Once she even told me, "Jennifer, I know it's hard what you're facing, and if you ever want to see a therapist about this stuff, it's okay."

I never did see a professional, but in retrospect, I believe that Mom's continual effort to pull herself away from her dysfunctional childhood played a fundamental role in my recovery. *If she has the strength to overcome her problems, I can overcome mine*, I thought.

My parents always encouraged us to talk about our feelings at home. They were adamant about enjoying time together as a family. Once in fifth grade, I asked to attend a three month long summer camp because my friends were doing it.

"Absolutely not," Dad said. "We don't want to rid ourselves of our kids!" At the time, I was thoroughly annoyed that I couldn't spend the summer with my friends, but I was glad to know my dad liked me so much he wanted me around.

After the accident, my strong, supportive family and their constant encouragement helped me work through my loss of self. This took time. Things were different for me than they were before my injury, and I hated it.

The only way I knew how to save the old Jennifer was to do the same things she'd always done. On February 28, 1995, a group of women met at 7:00 P.M. for our book club. The selection was *A Prayer for Owen Meany*, a well-written novel that should have grabbed me. This book is detailed, and widely recognized for dovetailing together perfectly. In fact, the first paragraph is legendary: "I am doomed to remember a boy with a wrecked voice—not because of his voice, or because he was the smallest person I ever knew..." But the words didn't capture me. Nothing held my attention for very long.

I remember trying to read the novel, sprawled across my bed, just thinking about past meetings—discussing literature, laughing about life, and chit-chatting. This memory didn't last long as my book fell to the floor with a thump, while my arms dangled over the bed. My eyes didn't feel tired, but my body felt limp. *I will just rest here for a few minutes until the limpness goes away.*

After a while, I picked up the book again, and stared at the front cover. *Why is the author's name, John Irving, printed in such a large font above the title?* My mom gave me the book two weeks earlier, and I tried several times to read it, but so far I'd made it through only half. At least I think I made it halfway, but I couldn't remember many details about what I read.

The meeting would begin in a few hours, and I wanted to read as much as possible, so I opened to the first page again. "I am doomed to remember a boy..." and I stopped. *Reading for book club is good practice for me*, I told myself, closing my eyes for just a second. *After all, soon I'll be reading and studying a lot when I get back to school*! I looked down at my book again. *What's it called?* I couldn't remember, so I peeked at the front cover and read the words: *A Prayer for Owen Meany. Who's Owen Meany?* Words just didn't stick inside my head. *Someone should invent Scotch tape for the brain.* I closed my eyes, pressing my fingers hard against my temples, hoping to stop my brain from pulsating.

"Jennifer, sweetheart, it is time to go to book club. Jennifer?" I guess I drifted off to sleep, and opened my eyes after hearing Mom repeat my name multiple times. "I'm sorry to wake you up, but we have to leave, Honey. Do you still want to go to book club?" she asked.

"Oh yeah, I'm up, I'm up," I said. "But Mom, I never finished reading the book."

"Don't worry, Jennifer, half the people never finish anyway," she said. "Let's go."

Walking outside during a Minnesota summer can sometimes feel like walking into a sauna because the air is so humid, you can taste it. It still felt good to be outside. I held onto my mom's arm until we got inside the car when I collapsed into the front seat.

I just looked out the window while she tried to talk to me. The sky was dark, and I wished I was still asleep in my bed, as a dense cloud of fatigue surrounded me.

When we reached the house for the meeting, my heart tingled with anticipation because I wasn't quite sure what to expect. As soon as I walked inside, I started to feel anxious from all the energy for me to absorb.

"Oh, Jennifer! It's wonderful to see you," Taia said, hugging me when we saw each other, being careful not to squeeze my neck too hard.

So many people. So many voices. So many choices for conversation. So many colors in the room. The spinning in my head got worse. My mom stood beside me, and other women came over to tell me how great I looked. In truth, I didn't feel so great. Not knowing how to respond, I just smiled and answered,

"Well you should have seen me a few months ago. I didn't look so good then."

It must have sounded funny to joke about a personal tragedy. In retrospect, I see my humor as a defense mechanism. I couldn't contribute much to a conversation about the book, but I could still smile a lot and make people laugh.

As we made our way into the living room, I grabbed the most comfortable-looking chair, so I wouldn't have to share space with anyone else. Again, I heard giggling, talking, and discussion about the book. I wished I could somehow pick just one person to talk to while everyone else vanished.

Despite what I thought about myself that night, I must have said something sensible because, later, Brent showed me a letter that Taia had sent to him:

Dear Brent,

I've been meaning to write for a while, and am finally prompted to because of last night's book club meeting. I was especially struck by Jennifer: she was animated, funny, engaged, and a full participant in the discussion. No one was affording her special treatment, no one hovered and I had the pleasure of seeing her enjoy herself. I realized that despite whatever pain, trauma, and long-term effects the accident has brought upon Jennifer, she will have happiness and success. She will achieve and contribute. I've always had the faith that Jennifer would overcome, but I saw my faith confirmed last night. So there you have it, all from a seemingly insignificant book club meeting!

Love,

Taia

My memory of the next two months is sparse, but I know life was anything but capricious. Every morning I went to the gym with my mom at 5:30 A.M., and walked on the treadmill. Every afternoon I napped and looked through photos of my study abroad. Every evening a different family member or friend came to visit me. My goal was to return to college as soon as I could, and it became my personal challenge to completely heal. Having little idea what kind of adjustments awaited me, I didn't anticipate that rehabilitation from a Traumatic Brain Injury would take a lifetime commitment.

5

Note to Self: Get *Scotch Tape* for Brain

Education is learning what you didn't even
know you didn't know.

~Daniel J. Boorstin

My parents hoped I'd be well-enough to return to college for fall
semester. But I wanted to return even earlier, in the spring. "I'm
not in the hospital anymore. I need to get back to my life!" I told
them. Brent had already returned to BYU, so he'd be there to
help me. "I'll live close to campus, so I won't have to walk far to
class," I said, firmly. I convinced my parents that I was ready to
handle college again and in April 1995, just eight months after
the accident, I boarded a flight for Utah.

I remember saying goodbye to the lush, green Minnesota
land and looking out the airplane window to say hello to the
golden, towering Wasatch Mountains. BYU is located in Provo, a
city filled with approximately 115,000 people, located 40 miles
south of Salt Lake City at the base of the Wasatch Mountains. Its
Western land looks much different than the Midwest I was
used to.

Once I felt the airplane wheels touch the ground in Salt Lake City, it seemed as if I'd never left Utah. I remembered a small reminder note my mom gave me, so I reached into my pocket to pull out a crumpled piece of paper and read, "Brent will be waiting for you outside the gate. Don't forget you have two suitcases to pick up at the baggage check."

There were bugs in my stomach as I walked down the hallway to the exit gate. It had been over one year since I'd lived in Provo, and I wondered how my life would be different than it was before my trip to Chile, and before my accident. As I exited the plane, I saw Brent waiting for me.

He's the perfect older brother, always available to support his family. Once a nurse in the hospital even said he was like my mother hen.

"Hi Jennifer! You look great! I'm so glad you're here!" My brother gave me a big hug.

"C'mon," I said. "Let's go get my bags. I have two bags," I said, as I showed him Mom's note, pleased that I remembered on my own.

My head felt thick again because not only was I nervous to be back at BYU, but I was cognitively exhausted from traveling between two noisy airports. I'd grown used to this feeling, so I just ignored it. Besides, my brother stood right beside me, so I wouldn't have to remember where I was or what I had to do.

We picked up my bags and made our way to Brent's car. He stood outside the door as I crawled into the front seat. "I already moved the seat back as far as it'll go," he explained. "Because I know you need to stretch your legs out." He was right. My knees did feel bruised and my hip pulsated, so it felt good to extend my legs.

As we pulled up to the apartment where I'd live for my last year at BYU, I looked out the window and wondered why it seemed like I had never left Provo. The streets of this small city still felt familiar to me. I couldn't wait to return to my life, and finally be back to normal.

Every doctor and nurse at the hospital warned me that college with a Traumatic Brain Injury would be challenging. *But, I'm different,* I told myself. *It won't be that tough for me. If I work hard enough, I can beat this.* Before the accident, academic perseverance had brought me success. If I wanted to do well on a test, I'd organize study groups to help me prepare, and I spent long hours at the library reviewing my notes.

But, things had changed. I couldn't focus on one topic for very long (which made reading difficult), and I constantly felt exhausted (which made studying at the library out of the question).

Since I was still certain I could handle it, I chose to sit in the front row on my first day back in class, like I always did. The course, called *Impressionism in the Arts,* was a requirement for my major. I assume the professor spent the first part of class describing course requirements, but I'm not sure. As much as I loved my major and studying the arts, I could only pay attention in short snippets. I do remember the second half when he talked about a beautiful Claude Monet painting called *The Rocks of Belle-Île.*

"Monet's remarkable series of paintings of the rocks and sea at Belle-Île astounded the Paris art world when he first showed them in 1887," the professor explained. I knew this was important, so I made sure my tape recorder worked. A nurse suggested I record all lectures to help me review my notes. Then, I started to write the date in my notebook, but I blanked. *What day is it again? This humanities class meets Monday, Wednesday, and Friday. Yesterday was Sunday so today must be Monday.* I peered over my neighbor's shoulder, hoping he had the date written on his paper. It said *May 8, 1995,* so I wrote this date on my page.

I listened to the professor still talking about Monet's work. *What exactly was he saying just before I'd written the date?* I couldn't remember. *Monet's work was first in a—what do you call it when you have a group of the same? I forgot the word he used. It's like a chain or a sequence. What word did he use?* I scrunched my eyes and pressed firmly on my temples. It was no use. I couldn't remember the word.

I looked up to focus back on the lecture and noticed we were on to the next Monet painting. I pushed the button on my tape recorder again to make sure it still worked. Recording lectures was a great way to pull me from situations like this one. Too often my thoughts were fleeting and if the professor said something important, by the time I looked down at my paper, the idea was gone. Again, I wished I had *Scotch tape* for my brain.

"*Series!*" I suddenly remembered the word I'd forgotten. *Monet's painting, Rocks at Belle-Île, was thought to be the first in a series of paintings!* I quickly jotted this down in my notes.

When the first test day came, I studied extra hard, even making flashcards to help me review. But, my nerves got the better of me, and I clammed up on the test. The first question asked, "Name the artist who painted *The Rocks of Belle-Île*." I couldn't remember, so I looked around the room for some sort of clue, such as a photograph of other impressionist paintings, or something to jolt my failing memory.

It was no use. My mind meandered along with my eyes, and I ended up thinking about whatever I was looking at and forgetting all about Monet. Besides, I had a much more difficult time grasping new information after my injury. Studying made my brain hurt, which made class painful. I did so poorly on the first exam that I just threw it in the garbage, so as not to remind me of my stupidity.

One day after class, I wandered into the BYU Writing Fellows Office, where I'd been a tutor before my accident. A Writing Fellow is assigned to work with a specific class and read 15–20 student papers twice a semester. After giving the students a written critique, we met with them to discuss their work. I was anxious to do this again because not only did I love it, but reentering the world I knew pre-injury seemed to give me a break from my head throbs. I didn't need to use as much brain power when I was in familiar territory.

There was nothing for me to do in the office that day—no appointments with students, and no papers to gather. So, I just looked around the room, staring at all the books, and at a corkboard on the wall with photos of all the tutors

One photo had our entire group seated together on a mid-sized cliff up at Brighton Resort, just east of Salt Lake City. I remembered feeling wonderful in that photo because the air was dry, the sun was bright, and we'd just returned from a hike around the resort. Plus, I was with my friends who also wanted to make an impact through their writing.

I tried to say aloud the first names of everyone seated on the cliff. "That's me!" I said, first pointing to myself. I had long hair in the picture, a few inches past my shoulders, but now I looked different because it was partially shaved so Dr. White could stitch my injury.

"Hi Jen," a voice interrupted my nostalgia. In walked Deirdre, our program director. She moved next to me, as if we were two patrons scrutinizing wall art at a gallery.

I started pointing to each photo and naming my friends. "And that's Brent, I know my brother. And that is… um…um…what's his name again?"

"That's Jon Jensen…and…there is John Welch," Deirdre answered my question, but I stopped her.

"Wait! Seriously, I have to try on my own, Deirdre. This is important to me. I need to remember who these people are." Feeling frustrated, I struggled for several minutes and came up with only three names on my own. Deirdre ended up giving me hints for the others. If she said their first name, I remembered the last name. It's as if I'd entered midway through the story of my life.

The fall 1995 Writing Fellows Orientation took place at Brighton Resort again, on September 2nd. It was the same location, but my experience wasn't the same. This time I waited on a couch in the cabin, and tried to rest while everyone else hiked because I knew it would be too physically taxing for me.

After the hike and after lunch, Deirdre asked the experienced Writing Fellows to sit on the stage, in front of everyone, and answer questions from the new tutors. I sat on the stage. Brent was there. Jon Jenson and John Welch both sat on the stage. I knew most everyone because they'd started the Writing Fellows program with me. I finally felt at ease, comfortable, back in my element.

"Tell us your favorite, most enlightening humorous experience as a first semester Writing Fellow," Deirdre requested. One-by-one, we shared stories and tutoring examples. I was second in line to speak, so I silently prepared a speech. I knew I needed to be funny. I needed to say something about writing. *Okay, um, before Chile. Funny students? Did I tutor any funny students? Silly papers that I edited?* I remembered meeting with some students, but nothing really funny.

John Welch finished his answer and I was next. My palms began to sweat. *What would I say? Writing. Writing. Writing is like, um...writing is like...skinny dipping!* All of a sudden, I remembered a poem I wrote called "Deep Thoughts." Although it had nothing to do with Writing Fellows, it was about writing; a spoof on the Saturday Night Live skit, which my generation loved.

When it was my turn, I decided to open with a pleasant greeting, before introducing myself and explaining that I'd begun as a Writing Fellow its first semester at BYU, and how I left for a study abroad in Chile. I thought I sounded clear and eloquent.

"And so I wrote this poem," I said. "Comparing writing to skinny dipping, you know...um, ah, like from that one show...what's it called?" I couldn't recall the three words which I'd remembered only moments before. I looked at Brent for clarification, but he had no idea where I was going.

"Jon? Do you remember that poem?" He gave me a blank stare too. I was on my own. "What's it called? Um...um... ah...oh. From that one comedy skit show, Brent? You know what I'm talking about. The one I always watched with Corinne, Steve, and Nick back in high school. What was it called?"

"Do you mean Saturday Night Live?" he asked.

"Yes!" and I let out a sigh of relief. "Saturday Night Live!"

I looked back at the audience. "Remember how they had that one skit on the show? Deep Thoughts or whatever? My poem was a deep thought comparing writing to skinny dipping." Everyone understood my comparison, and laughed, right along with me, just like I wanted. This disrupted my flow, caused me to stumble and forget what I'd been talking about again. I tried to cover up my sudden memory loss with, "ah…um…so…anyway," and I didn't sound so eloquent. "It was pretty funny," I said, since that was all I could remember.

In reality, I'd written the poem during my Freshman English class, more than a year before becoming a Writing Fellow, which is why neither Jon nor Brent had any idea what I was talking about.

"I think I still have the poem at home," I continued. "But it's on this practically shredded paper, with holes in it. I was in a car accident last year." I never had a problem remembering that I'd been in a car accident, and assumed everyone else wanted to hear about it, so I mentioned it any chance I got. "Most of my papers were destroyed, but somehow this poem about writing survived intact," I smiled as I told my story, trying to make light of something serious. "So writing is like skinny dipping or something like that. Anyway…um…so anyway." I lost my train of thought again, and didn't know what else to say. Jon, seated next in line, must have caught on to my confusion because he immediately started talking.

When the presentations were over, I saw a small staircase at stage right. Most people scurried down the steps or jumped off. But, I hesitated because I saw double when I looked down, another result of my injury. My head throbbed from trying to recall events from my past. *Why was I here, again? How long was this conference supposed to last?* I felt so tired. I longed to just curl up in a quiet closet someplace and hide. I saw Jon a few strides before me, about to go down the staircase.

"Jon! Wait," I pleaded. "Let me hang on to your shoulder when I go down the stairs." My brain shut off after stressful, memory-testing situations like the one I was in, so I don't remember much more about the conference after that.

Later at home, I found the short poem again:
Writing is like skinny dipping
At first it takes a lot of guts
But once you do it you feel cool and tingly
You just have to jump in
It's not all that embarrassing
After you've tried it a bunch of times

While sitting in my apartment living room, I reflected that life with a brain injury is similar to skinny dipping. It's extremely embarrassing and it takes a lot of guts. My injury affected my cognitive functioning, I was easily distracted, irritated by noise, and my short-term memory was terrible. Trying to remember my past and paying attention during class weren't my only struggles as a brain injured college student. My social life was different too.

One night I went to a dance club about 60 minutes north of Provo with my roommate, Candace, and three guys. In retrospect, I should have predicted the experience to be draining, since I remember feeling disoriented the entire drive there. But, I used to like crowds and noise, so I figured I'd enjoy myself. My head spun; the walls trembled and it was so dark that I couldn't see anything inside the club. I felt dizzy and despondent about dancing. My heart raced faster as the noise pounded louder. It was scary. I imagined myself trampled by a crowd of drunks, and getting injured enough to go back to the hospital. My eyes started to blur and I needed a break.

Suddenly, I had a déjà-vu experience, as if I'd been at this place before. Something felt familiar. But, it was my first time at the club, so I didn't understand the feeling. I tried to push my way through the crowd, in search of an escape.

"Oh, excuse me. Excuse me," I apologized to everyone after bumping into them. I wanted to find a table, but my friends pulled me to the middle of the dance floor and started jumping from side to side, arms flaying, and heads bopping to the beat of the music. I danced a little more, but felt silly with my lack of rhythm.

"Excuse me, excuse me," I said again, bumping shoulders as I looked around for an empty chair off the dance floor. I pushed my way to the first table I saw, as if it was Utopia. An unfamiliar man already sat there, but I didn't care. I took a seat anyway.

"Having fun, Jen?" the stranger asked. At first I wondered how he knew my name. But, then I remembered he drove me to the club.

"No, I'm not having fun," I answered him with a scowl on my face. Everything in the room blared. The music was too loud. There were too many people and too many colors. The commotion made my head spin. I just looked down at the table and wondered how to stop myself from crying.

Then the déjà-vu hit again. I realized I was remembering a very specific experience in Chile. One time my friends and I went to a dance club, called *La Oz*, really late. It was almost 1:00 A.M. when we arrived, but the lights, the crowd, and the lively Latin music energized me. We stayed until after 4:00 A.M. We danced into the wee hours of the morning, several nights per week, on my study abroad. In fact, I barely ever slept. Very often I'd stay up late studying, then I'd go out dancing, and then I would get up early for class.

There wasn't much time for sleep the night after *La Oz* because our bus left for Valparaíso at 8:30 the next morning. Our group went to visit the house of Pablo Neruda, who is considered one of the greatest and most influential Chilean poets of the 20th century. I remember his house was beautiful, right on the coast, and he had a magnificent collection of everything from preserved butterflies to hand-made pottery. Our Study Abroad directors, Dr. Hilda Rojas and her husband Dr. Gonzalo Rojas, knew him very well. In fact, we saw a huge yellow shoe, which they gave him, resting in his bar room. Dr. Rojas said she saw it at a shoe repair shop and liked it. New information and crowds of people were electrifying to me back then.

But, I didn't feel like this anymore. The vigor in the dance club this time just zapped me. I needed something to focus on, so I gazed at my bare wrist and realized I'd forgotten to wear a watch. My head still spun, but somehow I found the strength to force a smile to the man sitting at the table.

"Are you okay?" he asked.

"Yeah, it's a headache. I just feel a little sick," I lied. Really it was the noise and the commotion making my head spin and my thigh muscles throb. *Why did my friend suggest that we come here anyway?* I wondered in frustration. *She knows about my car accident! She knows that I broke my legs! How did she think I could dance?*

"That's too bad you have a headache," the man interrupted. "I'm feeling sick too, so that's why I'm not dancing, but, it looks like fun." Again, I forced a smile on my face before swallowing the lump in my throat. I couldn't wait to go home.

I don't even remember leaving the club that night, but I do remember collapsing on my bed at home. The burning around my legs and inside my head was almost unbearable. I lay motionless, forever exhausted, yet I struggled to fall asleep. Everything was silent in the room except for the chattering inside my head. *Stop talking stupid brain. Go to sleep. Why can't I go to sleep? How much time has passed?* I lifted my head and squinted to read the time on the clock: 2:00 A.M. *Oh, I'm so tired. I feel sick.* My never-ending fatigue must have been too much because after a few hours, eventually I fell sleep.

When I woke the next morning, I just lay still as I tried to think of a reason to get up. It's like I hadn't slept a wink all night. This combined with my painful dance club experience was little motivation to do anything other than just lie there. Besides, it was Saturday and I had nothing to do. I hated the way I was feeling as much as I hated my injury.

Leaning over my bed, I grabbed my phone off the floor and dialed my parent's phone number. I was relieved when I heard my mom's voice at the other end say, "Hi, honey! How are things?"

"I dunno. I didn't sleep well, so I'm pretty tired."

"How did it go last night?"

Such a simple, yet poignant question and I didn't know how to answer. *Last night? What did I do last night?* I could only think about what was right before me. The only thing I knew was that I lay in my bed. I couldn't remember last night, so I didn't speak.

"Jennifer? Are you still there?"

"Yeah, I'm here. Mom, I can't remember last night."

"Okay, I think you told me you were going dancing in Salt Lake with Candace."

"Oh yeah, Salt Lake!" I remembered everything and my description came flooding. "We drove up with these three guys. I don't remember their names, but I shouldn't have gone because I was dead-tired. There were so many people and I can't dance anymore; my legs just don't bend like they should. I sat there at a table and there were a bunch of drunk people around. They were slam dancing. It was crazy…and…so…well, um, whatever." I stumbled and my voice slowed. "I don't know, um, I was tired." I stopped talking and felt my thoughts disintegrate. *What exactly was my point again?*

My mom caught on to my brain freeze, and changed the subject. "Well, I hope you can get some sleep tonight." We chatted for a bit longer, but I was too tired to say much more.

Sometimes I wonder if my injured brain just got lazy. Words and thoughts entered, but after realizing there wasn't much room, they just wandered around into oblivion. I don't know which was worse that night: the fact that I was too tired to even speak to my mom or the fact that I lost track of my thoughts mid-sentence. All this confusion happened inside my brain where others couldn't see. The hardest part was that I looked better than I felt, so people often forgot about my injury, and thought I was doing better than I was.

My mom once used a great analogy. "It's like when someone dies," she said. "People are there until after the funeral, and then they can go on with their lives. Basically, it's the family that's left feeling the pain."

It was impossible for me not to feel shafted about my injury at some level. Life wore me out. I battled two extremes in everything I did: always studying and continually reviewing my notes, but barely passing some classes. I always felt exhausted, yet never slept through the night. I tried to hang out with friends and tried to do well, just as I did before my accident. But, I no longer had the same stamina I did before my accident.

6

Note to Self: You Have a Disability

If only we could pull out our brain
and use only our eyes.

~Pablo Picasso

At first, I tried to hide my memory problems and low energy. I pretended I felt fine during class when really I was overloaded and bombarded because so many people were spitting out information faster than I could process it. I didn't say anything to my professors about my injury, even when my grades suffered. I made the erroneous assumption that everything would just become easier over time, including school. If a brain injury was going be part of my life forever, then I figured I needed to learn to deal with it, alone.

Brent told me something that transformed my perspective. He suggested I register with the Office for Students with Disabilities to see if they could help. At first I was shocked by his idea. *I can't believe Brent thinks I have a disability. I mean, I don't have a wheelchair, and I'm not missing any limbs. I'm not blind. College is difficult for everyone; why should I expect anything special just because I'm struggling? I need to work harder, that's all.* I didn't know what this office could do for me, since I didn't see myself as disabled, but I went ahead and made an appointment anyway.

The small office was located in the basement of the tallest building on campus, and looked quickly thrown together with orange carpeting and a few cubicles. In spite of this, the staff was warm and encouraging. They understood exactly how to help me. The counselor I met with could tell right away that I wasn't open to any assistance.

"As much as you don't want to admit it," she said, "Jennifer, you now have a physical disability. Under The Rehabilitation Act of 1973, you are eligible to certain accommodations at school."

I thought about my experience taking the *Impressionism in the Arts* test. There were so many words and so many people in the room, I couldn't focus. I couldn't remember anything I'd studied, or even the purpose of the exam. I thought it was just because the injury had ruined my brain.

This was only partially true. My brain was permanently injured, and that wasn't going to change. But, it certainly wasn't ruined. It did, however, leave me saying "I can't" a lot. I can't be around large crowds because too many people and loud noises mean too much brain stimulation. I can't always find the words I want to use. I can't sleep through the night. I can't pay attention while reading books or listening in class. The disability office helped me understand that help was available for this and there was nothing wrong with needing accommodations to manage my injury.

"Jennifer, with some adjustments, the words 'I can't' will change to 'I can.' I'll need to see your medical records, but typically, students with a brain injury are given extended time on tests, as well as a distraction-free room for test-taking. Hopefully these accommodations will help you focus, and your hard work will pay off."

I called my mom later that night and asked her to send all the records from my hospital stays in Nebraska and Minnesota. I gave this information to the disability office, and they wrote a letter describing the necessary accommodations. It explained that a Traumatic Brain Injury left me with short-term memory loss and difficulty staying focused.

My counselor suggested I personally approached each of my professors and say, "I have a Traumatic Brain Injury," which were daunting words that tripped me up every time. It's as if I couldn't even speak English when I talked about my brain injury. I even practiced in front of the mirror at home before my first confrontation.

"I haf a Dramatic Brai-indery," I said, looking at my reflection. I tried to speak more slowly the second time. "I – have – a Traumatic Brainindery." The third time I moved my mouth in an even slower motion, and said, "I – have – a – Trau-mat-ic Br-aaaain-Innn-juuurrr-eee." I thought it sounded almost normal.

As soon as I got the words out, I went to Dr. Snyder's office to present the letter and tell him I – have – a – Trau-mat-ic Br-aaaain-Innn-juuurrr-eee. He was my favorite English professor, from whom I'd already taken a class, and now I'd signed up for *Literature of the American West* with him. I was excited about the class, but nervous about the letter. I felt like it gave me authorization to be a charity case, and I couldn't imagine how he'd handle it.

When I gave him the letter, he quickly read it and said, "This is easy, Jennifer!"

I couldn't believe his pleasant reaction. "Easy? What will you do?"

He said I could take the tests home and do them at my own pace, on my own computer. Only the daily quiz, given for the previous day's reading assignment, would be a problem. He promised to give me these early and, again, I could do them home.

Almost every other BYU professor was willing to accommodate my needs, so I could manage my deficits better. I took tests in a private room without distractions. I also still recorded all lectures to listen again after class. Some professors even let me use notes during tests, or write a paper in place of a test. In retrospect, I wish I understood the accommodations available to me earlier, and confronted my *Writing About the Visual Arts* professor in the same way. I'm positive I would have done better in the class.

College tested my endurance, but I finished in April 1996, one class short from graduation as I had to return home for a final surgery. My orthopedic surgeon in Minneapolis wanted to remove the steel rods he'd placed inside my fractured femur bones because they'd healed completely, and if I was in another accident, my bone could dangerously shatter around the rod.

Bedridden, I spent the summer completing my final class through independent study to officially receive my bachelor's of arts degree in August 1996. Brent and I graduated together, standing side-by-side during the cap and gown ceremony, where I heard my mom scream, "Yeah, Brent and Jennifer!" It was the same moment that flashed before her, that morning in Nebraska, while she looked in the bathroom mirror.

7

Note to Self: Don't Forget Graduate School

The highest result of education is tolerance.

~Helen Keller

British Author Arthur Koestler once said that creativity is a type of learning process where the teacher and pupil are located in the same individual. Since I was bedridden from May until August, I spent those months both as pupil, completing my independent study class, and as teacher by reviewing a GRE (Graduate Record Examination) preparation book.

Education was extremely important to me and I wanted to continue on to graduate school. This meant I needed good GRE scores. When I returned to college after the accident, I assumed that over-preparing for exams would position me to do at least average work. Sometimes this theory worked. Often it did not. But, I tried the same thing and read page after page of the GRE prep book. I'd read and read, but couldn't recall anything just moments after I finished. Thus, I never scored well on any practice test, but this didn't deter me.

Several months later, I registered to take the GRE at the University of Minnesota with stars in my eyes. I didn't tell the registrar about my injury, nor did I ask for any accommodations; not only because I didn't know what was available, but because I didn't want to admit I needed help.

The university is gigantic and stretches across two cities, so I scribbled the directions to the testing site on a piece of paper, and I even did a test run. On exam day, I barely made it on time. Frantically running, I found an empty seat in the middle of the room. The test was long and many of the specifics are hazy.

I do remember that each question required a connection speed that I didn't have. *Compare two words. Fill in the blanks.* I could hardly remember what I wanted to say in less stressful situations. How could I remember words at that moment? Questions such as: "We never believed that he would resort to...in order to achieve his goal; we always regarded him as a...man." Pick the correct words:

A. Charm...insincere
B. necromancy...pietistic
C. logic...honorable
D. prestidigitation...articulate
E. subterfuge...honest

Just like during my *Impressionism in the Arts* class, I couldn't focus when I took the exam. Instead, I watched everyone in the room as thoughts meandered through my brain. *I'm supposed to pick which words go in the dotted lines, I guess. I'm so tired it's like I've forgotten how to think. I wonder what I'll do for dinner tonight. Should I study art history or English in grad school? The GRE is like taking the ACT in high school, only worse. That guy across the room looks so stressed. Everything in my head feels thick. Who cares about this test? I don't know the answers anyway, so I'll just make a design with my bubbles. As long as everything is filled out, it'll be fine. I need a nap.*

After I finished, I got up and handed my bubble sheet to the exam monitor. "Wow you must be a fast test-taker," he said. I guess; I'd only used ¾ of the time allotted. I looked down at my bubble design, and wondered how many answers I got correct.

When I received my test scores in the mail, several weeks later, I read the computer-generated score report and my heart sank. My random design wasn't a success after all. I barely got any answers correct. Five years before my car accident, I'd taken the ACT college-entrance exam and scored above the 90th percentile in the verbal section. Now, after the accident, I'd scored in the 14th percentile.

I'd played teacher as a Writing Fellow, and I was great at playing pupil. But, things were different now. What could I do? I felt empty and lost, as if my life was without purpose. I hated the way I felt, so I tried to pep-talk myself away from this self-deprecation. *Maybe I just need to learn to love and accept this new stupid person I've become. My life is not so bad. I may not have a job and I can't sleep at night, but I do have friends, even though I can't really do much with them since I'm so tired all the time.*

My pep-talk wasn't helping. I decided to walk aimlessly around the St. Paul, Minnesota neighborhood where I was living at the time. St. Paul is described as a somewhat bookish brother to Minneapolis because it has several liberal arts colleges and is more traditional than its twin city. Everything feels more old-school to me in St. Paul. Neighborhoods are full of large Victorian homes, tiny cafés and small book stores. My apartment was just a few blocks from The University of St. Thomas. I always watched students there studying on the grass, or fervently racing to class. It had been almost four years since I was an undergraduate and since my accident, and I craved to once again be a part of this atmosphere.

Not long after this neighborhood walk, I met with the master's of English department director to find out how I could enroll in his program. I explained that I'd graduated from BYU with a bachelor's degree in humanities and English. "My GRE

scores are not reflective of my abilities. I'm a terrible test-taker,"
I admitted. He assured me that other factors are equally important
for university acceptance—especially letters of recommendation
and undergraduate performance. Then I said something that
surprised me.

"I haf a Dramatic Brai-indery," the words blurted out so
fast I'm surprised he understood. "I was in a car accident."

"I'm sorry to hear that. Okay, what does that mean for the
program?" he asked.

"Oh, um, well, I need more time on tests." I repeated what
I'd learned from the BYU disabilities office about how to survive
college with a TBI: tape record lectures, more time on tests
(forgetting that I already told him that one), and I get overloaded
easily. "But I can do it!" I promised. He suggested I register as a
non-degree seeking student, and take one class in the program to
see if I could handle it.

The first course I registered for was *Introduction to
Composition Theory* with Dr. Michael Bellamy. Class met one
night per week from 6:00 – 9:00. In order to prepare, I spent the
entire morning on the first day reminding myself of what college
was like. I opened my old BYU photo album and looked through
old textbooks. Since I'd already taken writing courses as an
undergraduate, I thought I knew what to expect.

That evening I sat amongst other students, pretended I
was listening and laughed if another student told a joke. I fit right
in, and no one had any idea I was different. One man announced
he was 22 years old and just graduated from the University of
Wisconsin at Madison with an undergraduate degree in English.
This interested me only because many of my high school friends
went to the University of Wisconsin. I don't remember anything
else from the first day other than my head felt heavy and I was
tired.

We were supposed to read several selected articles about
writing theory in the class, and write 700-word analytical
responses to our reading. Seven-hundred words are about two
pages in length, so I was glad our assignments were short. I

looked at my syllabus, and noticed that we were to read *Rhetoric and Reality: Writing Instruction in American Colleges* by James Berlin. It took me an entire week to read what probably took other students only a couple hours. But, I loved the reading.

My favorite section was called "The Revival of Rhetoric," which discussed invention as it related to writing. I remembered my first Honors Intensive Writing class at BYU with Deirdre when she wrote a quote on the board from Lao Tsu that said, "Blessings come from adversity." We were asked to freewrite using an experience from our own life. I immediately thought to use this as an example of inventive writing for my analytical response. It had the right amount of analysis combined with personal experience; just what Dr. Bellamy wanted.

The next week, he handed back our work. Nothing was written on my first page, so I turned to the second and saw four simple words: "Jennifer, please see me." I wondered what he didn't like about my writing. Did I use too much passive voice or not enough big words?

After class, I approached Dr. Bellamy and, with a confused look, showed him my paper. "Jennifer," he spoke frankly, "You wrote about the wrong assignment."

"Oh…ah, sorry…thanks," I said, and I scurried out of the room. I felt ridiculous and assumed the professor just thought I was stupid. He didn't know about my brain injury, so he probably wondered what I was doing in graduate school in the first place. If nothing else, this was exactly what I thought.

"I'm not cut out for this," I told myself. I was glad I registered as a non-degree seeking student for my first class because, although I did finish *Introduction to Composition Theory*, I quickly decided not to continue in the program.

8

Note to Self: You're Not Stupid

The chief function of the body
is to carry the brain around.

~Thomas A. Edison

"I feel so stupid," I said.

My mom's reassuring look reminded me that no matter what, I'd already made her and my dad proud. Even if my recovery stopped, if this was it and I wasn't going to get any better, it was okay because I'd made so much progress. Friends and family always told me my accident could have been worse. They meant it could have killed me...it's a miracle I could even walk now...I could be paralyzed...I could have never returned to college. They were right, it could have been worse, but some days I think about how it could have been better, and how my life would be so much easier without a brain injury.

The car accident was more than 2000 days earlier, but I still needed to meet with a neuropsychologist to monitor my progress. My drive to The Minneapolis Clinic of Neurology on January 12, 1998 should have been easy: North on 169, east on

494, and two miles to Highway 100, almost passing my junior high school, and nine miles to the Duluth Street exit. It's a 20 minute drive from my parent's house, through familiar territory, and I'd traveled each road multiple times. But, after testing my mental limits in college, I knew not to trust my memory. I needed a cheat sheet, so I wrote the directions on scrap paper just in case.

I almost made it to the clinic trouble-free. A drive on the highway meant little variation: travel straight for a few miles, and the same speed almost the entire way. It wasn't until I reached the Duluth Street exit that I became perplexed. I was multitasking in unfamiliar territory: deciding which street, looking at names of street signs, turning either right or left, all while remembering the name of my destination.

I felt tired and nervous. I didn't sleep well the night before, which shouldn't surprise me because I rarely slept well. *It's not like this doctor can tell me anything I don't already know! I have a Traumatic Brain Injury. I have a disability. I'm slower now. I'm a miracle. Stupid car accident.* Feeling tired and frustrated, I pulled off the road and looked down at my directions. *Turn right onto Duluth Street exit/County Road – 66. What's County Road 66? Is it called Duluth Street or County Road 66?*

After muddling my way around what felt like a tangled cobweb, I stopped at a large, brown building with strange windows. It didn't look like an office building, but "The Minneapolis Clinic of Neurology" was labeled on the front door, so I knew this was the place. I walked in just in time for my appointment with a neuropsychologist, Dr. Steven Morgan.

Dr. Morgan asked me questions and administered a battery of tests to assess my memory, word retrieval, and intelligence, including the Halstead-Reitan Neuropsychological Test for Adults. This test measures brain dysfunction with problem solving, manual dexterity, and spatial variation. It was especially difficult for me because I couldn't take notes or ask questions during the test. Dr. Morgan placed me in front of a foam board full of holes cut into various shapes. He had me place corresponding shaped blocks into the holes, while blind-folded. This part was fairly easy, easy until he asked me to draw the block's location from memory, and then I struggled.

He also tested my capacity to simultaneously maintain two separate cognitive tasks. My performance on this test fell within the low-average range, which meant my ability to multitask had declined. Dr. Morgan said that although I'd made a strong recovery after a severe injury, there was evidence of residual cerebral dysfunction, especially in relation to my pre-injury abilities. My aptitude was defined between my pre-injury self and my post-injury self. It was difficult to reconcile these two people.

I also completed the MMPI-II test (Minnesota Multiphasic Personality Inventory-2™). This test asks a series of questions and uses validity scales to indicate whether the patient responded truthfully or was trying to manipulate the test. Some people want to appear normal (or abnormal), and choose what they believe are the "correct" answers.

The test results told me everything I didn't want to hear. I lacked skills in concentration, and my fine motor skills were impaired. For example, although I'm right handed, my finger-tapping speed was faster with my left hand than with my right. I performed below average on motor-speed, below average on concentration, and below average on visual-spatial construction. Dr. Morgan established that there was a "generalized decline in attention and concentration." I was easily distracted in higher-level reasoning. Although I was far from nonfunctioning, I was also far from the intellectual efficiency of a college graduate. This made it official; I was forever impaired. In addition to a damaged brain, if there was a test for a damaged heart, my scores would have been off the charts. I felt worthless. How would I function?

To my surprise, Dr. Morgan had a different perception of my injury and he wrote the following analysis:

While the effects of her brain injury may not be noticeable when confronted with more routine familiar tasks, she will be slower and less efficient when dealing with demands, under time pressure, or under stressful conditions. Despite this, Jennifer is a woman with very pleasant, efficient interpersonal skills, a great drive and she maximizes her strengths. Although her higher level verbal/language skills are reduced relative to her pre-morbid level, she nonetheless presents well conversationally, has excellent work habits and has learned many useful compensatory skills.

This analysis gave me a glimmer of hope. Although I was slower and less efficient than I was pre-injury, maybe with compensation, I could still accomplish the same goals. The problem was that, in spite of the lessons I learned from the disability office at BYU, I still wasn't very good at recognizing when I needed help and how to ask for it.

9

Note to Self: Just Get on With Life

Travel and change of place impart new
vigor to the mind.

~Seneca

I refused to let a brain injury conquer me, and this glimmer of
hope was all I needed to create my next big adventure. Several
months later I found a program based out of Utah which sent
college-age students to teach English in China. *This is the type of
thing I need. A new culture, a new experience will make a new
me*, I told myself. It didn't take long for me to call the program's
office to set up an informational meeting with one of their staff
members.

At the meeting, I learned that I was older than the
previous teachers in the program. Typically, students ages 19 to
21 participated as summer interns, after their second year or third
year of college, but I was almost 24 and had already graduated
from college. As long as this didn't bother me, he said I'd be a
great addition to their program. I chose not to say anything about
my brain injury during this meeting because I didn't want to

scare him by using the words "brain" and "injury" in the same sentence.

I did what needed to be done in order to get to China. I applied for a new passport, got the recommended vaccinations, and bought *The Lonely Planet China* travel guide, until everything came together. Months later, I found myself sitting with my back pressed up against an airport wall in Korea waiting for two hours to board a flight to Guangzhou, China where I'd teach at a small elementary school for six months. The two hours was enough time to get my passport stamped and to take a nap.

I have to get my passport stamped. I have to get my passport stamped. I repeated this chant over and over in my head for fear that if I stopped, I'd forget. But, after 20 hours in the air, I felt like my head was on fire. It hurt just thinking about my deep exhaustion, so I tried to think about something else. *I totally can't believe I'm going to China. What am I thinking, going to China? I can't believe I'm doing this. I'm so tired. I have to get my passport stamped.* More than anything, I just wanted to make the world stop for a minute—so I tossed my backpack against the wall, and plopped onto the floor.

I must have drifted in and out of sleep for more than 90 minutes until I heard someone rapidly scurrying by, so close to me that I got a whiff of their bowl of Korean Noodles. It startled me at first, until I realized where I was.

"Hey, come on, we're leaving!" A girl in my teaching group tapped my shoulder with her toe before rushing off to the gate. She was the one in my group with whom I'd connected the most. I liked her. Her style reminded me of my urban friends back home in Minneapolis. We'd had a few earlier conversations about how she loved college as much as I did, and she'd already lived in China for one year while her dad taught at a Chinese university. Unlike your typical ultra-conservative Utahn, she was a little edgy, which I also liked.

At that moment, I couldn't remember her name so I just said, "thanks."

I followed nameless girl onto the airplane. When we got to our seats, another man from our group looked at me, smiled and asked, "Oh did you get enough sleep? Because you have a sleep mark on your forehead." He chuckled as if he'd caught me in an embarrassing act.

I wondered if I really did have a mark after sleeping for so long on the floor. But, after rubbing my forehead, I figured out that he was just talking about the scar on my forehead.

"No, that's a scar," I informed him. I probably sounded irritated by his comment, and I was.

"Oh, um, sorry," he said. I didn't give any more detail, and I think he was the one who felt embarrassed. Suddenly, I realized that I never got my passport stamped. I was disappointed, but there was nothing I could do, so I just sat down in my assigned seat. I relaxed when I saw I was seated next to nameless girl.

"Sorry, what's your name again?" she asked. "I never forget a face, but I'm terrible with names."

She thinks she's bad with names? If she only knew about my brain injury. "Yeah me too," I answered. "My name's Jennifer."

"I'm Kathryn, in case you forgot."

I was glad she told me, and I repeated it in my head over and over again in hopes that it would somehow stick. *Kathryn. Kathryn. Kathryn.* It was another time where I wished someone had invented *Scotch Tape* for the brain.

Somewhere in the space between Korea and Hong Kong, I captured one hour of worthless sleep. I felt horrible. My body ached for rest after sitting in an airplane for so long, combined with the throbbing headache feeling of a brain injury. I couldn't sleep and wanted to throw-up. This made me feel even worse because I knew I'd have to expend more energy doing that.

Kathryn became a close friend during our six months together. We constantly talked about our college classes, her two boyfriends who both wanted to marry her, and how neither of us could believe we'd be in China for six months. We talked about everything—everything except my brain injury.

One time the director asked me, "Why do you have all those scars on your legs?" I told him I broke my legs in a car accident, but didn't see any reason to tell him anything else. By telling people about the brain injury, I thought I'd be making excuses for my limits, and I hate excuses more than limits. I knew I'd just have to work harder at what seemed easy for everyone else.

After the airplane landed in Hong Kong, we caught a ferry into Guangzhou, and a bus into Panyu, the region that I'd call home for the next six months. We had one week to familiarize ourselves with the neighborhood, and to assemble our lesson plans for the next teaching week. There was work to do, but jetlag had sunk in, so rather than go anywhere, I just lay in my bed. I got up only to eat and use the bathroom.

I always wanted to fall asleep but never could, so I usually just wrote in my journal:

> *I'm feeling so tired and lethargic. I know this is jetlag, but I usually feel like this even when I'm not traveling. A brain injury is like continuous jetlag. The thing is jetlag goes away once your body readjusts, but I doubt if my body will ever readjust from this annoying brain injury.*

Eventually I did cycle in and out of sleep, and something normalized for me. By day five (I think it was day five, but I can't be certain), Kathryn and a few others wanted to take the ten minute bus ride into Shiqiao, the closest big city to the school. We walked around this small town together.

"Hey, Kathryn, I really need to use the bathroom," I said, after a while. "I wonder if that bookstore over there has some real toilets." I was tired of squatting in a private corner on the street, so I got out my translation book, turned to the part about asking for a bathroom, and went up to the girl behind the front desk.

"Is there a public toilet nearby?" I read the words loudly, in broken Chinese, as if she'd be able to understand me the louder I spoke. I tried to use proper tones, but I think I was way off, so I just showed the girl my book, and pointed to the phrase.

"Oh, you good," she said, emphasizing the last word, grinning. Then she took me outside, around the corner to a "real" toilet. She left and I took care of my personal business.

When I finished, I walked back around the corner to look for this girl so I could thank her, and saw she'd been waiting for me the entire time. "Name Ying," she said, as she pointed her thumb to her chest and quickly rattled off three complicated Chinese words. I only caught the word *Ying*. I also heard something that sounded like *kuh*.

All the native Chinese teachers at our school had American names, so I wondered if she'd like an American name too. Kuh sounded like Kim. "I'll call you Kim, okay? Kim is your American name."

"Kim?" she smiled. I'm sure she was excited about the idea of having an American name. She hugged me and said, "I love you."

Kathryn ran from the store, yelling, "Jennifer! I think that was the last one," pointing to a bus pulling away. I quickly waved goodbye to my new friend Kim, and we chased after it, running as fast as we could.

It was no use. We couldn't catch up to the bus. I got nervous, and crazy thoughts ran through my head. *No one in China knows I'm brain injured. I could do something stupid. What if we get separated and I forget the name of where we're staying? I don't know the language. I'm so tired. Would Kathryn find it weird if I lie down and take a nap right here in the street? How am I going to get home?* It was late. My eyes stung and my head throbbed. Kathryn turned around and must have seen the terror in my eyes.

"Jennifer, it's not a big deal. There are other ways to get around besides the bus. Let's try a motorcycle taxi." She nodded to two men waiting next to their motorcycles on the side of the road. The men revved their throttles and steered in our direction.

One got off his bike to talk to us. He looked like a wrinkly grandfather. "Need ride? You have Chinese Yuan or American Dollar?"

"We'll give you two American Dollars," Kathryn insisted.

The wrinkly man turned to the other man and said, "Ahhhhh!"

"Okay, how about five dollars?" Kathryn offered.

The men tried to get us to pay $15 then $12. We did the "Ahhhhh!" response, which is the Chinese nasal snarl to show we thought it was too much money, just like the men did. "Too expensive," Kathryn told them, in Chinese. We turned away and walked off. The men followed until we agreed to pay them $11 for both of us. Kathryn and I turned to look at one another, grinned, and then hopped onto the motorcycles.

The wind felt exhilarating blowing against my skin all the way home. As soon as we got inside, not saying a word to Kathryn, I went upstairs and I fell into my bed.

10

Note to Self: Did I Make the Right Decision?

> I would like to spend the whole of my life traveling if I could borrow another life to spend at home.
>
> ~William Hazlitt

When we finally began teaching, I felt up for the task because the summer before college I worked as a teaching assistant at an elementary school in Minneapolis. My students there had already completed first grade, but were behind on their reading skills and most had behavioral problems. I helped them improve enough to advance to second grade. To do so, I spent the first part of every class reading to the kids. I thought my job in China would be the same.

The Chinese school's philosophy was that children learn through action, so we prepared lessons and activities that focused on verbs, things the kids could do: *I am, I go,* and *I feel.* I was assigned to teach three and four year olds for the summer, but, frankly, it felt more like babysitting. The kids were rambunctious and not interested in our lessons.

My first week was tough. I did the same thing I'd done with the elementary students in Minneapolis—read books. But this time it didn't work as well. One day, I pulled up a chair and held up *Harold and the Purple Crayon* by Crockett Johnson. Some of the kids ran around the room, so I predictably yelled, "Kids sit down!" pointing to the floor in front of me. Everyone plopped down except for a boy named Deng Qiao Feng.

This child was extremely creative and seemed to understand connections far beyond the normal capacity of a four-year-old. He wasn't able to say very many English words, but he understood everything we said. However, he was a wild child, touching everything and running around the room, which made teaching him and the other students very difficult.

When he finally sat down, I started talking in my best child-like voice. "Okay kids," I said. "Today we're going to learn about the word 'go.' Can you say that word, 'go'?"

I held up the book and started reading. *One evening Harold decided to go for a walk in the moonlight. But there wasn't any moon, and Harold needed a moon for a walk in the moonlight. Fortunately, he brought his purple crayon...*I stopped. No one was listening.

"Kids, kids! Look at me." Then I watched Deng Qiao Feng run off. Another kid followed him. Two girls sprawled themselves out on the floor, and one boy started chattering in Chinese to another child. I didn't know how to get them to stay in one place for longer than five seconds, and I wished I'd slept better at night because my head pounded from all the screeching voices. I was about to start screaming myself, and just then Ben walked in.

Ben was the school's Chinese principal. I think he understood English, but I rarely heard him speak. I wasn't sure if this was because he didn't have much language confidence or simply because he was a man of very few words. He came into my classroom, sat down on a chair, and saluted me. Suddenly, I panicked. I didn't know what to do, so I repeatedly told the kids to come back to the reading area. But, as soon as I opened the book again, another kid would do something disruptive and I'd have to grab them. There were too many scrambling bodies for me to handle. I felt like I was going to lose my mind.

I knew that Ben watched me lose control, and I wanted to redeem myself. So, after class I looked over to where he sat, only to see him scurry out of the room before I could do anything.

It didn't matter. *What's done is done*, I thought. Nothing mattered to me at that point, except for the fact that I wanted to be alone, without a bunch of noisy children around. Besides, it was stifling in the school. *How did they expect us to be good teachers when it was so muggy? Ever heard of air conditioning? This place is stupid. But, then again, I'm stupid too. Just reading to the kids? That wasn't creative or skillful. Of course they didn't want to pay attention to English words when they couldn't understand the language.* These feelings just aggravated me more. I knew something had changed inside of me. I used to be so patient with children, and now I just wanted to strangle one.

After teaching for three weeks, our group took a weekend trip to Yangshuo, a town located in the Guangxi Province, which borders Vietnam. The few people in our group who had been there before referred to this place as the "Cancun of China." Many foreigners visited because it's a paradise for rock climbing, mountain biking, and kayaking. You can also rent bicycles to ride around town, take Chinese cooking classes, and even visit a restaurant called *Planet Yangshuo*. The name is on a blue sign with red lettering, replicating the *Planet Hollywood* American restaurant and bar. Yangshuo is complete with little cafes, shops, and travel agencies.

We walked into one of these agencies shortly after checking into a hotel to set up a tour to the town's Buddha Caves. The strong draw to these caves is its curative mud bath. The idea of a mud bath sounded wonderful to me, but I was wary of any sort of cave because I struggled with claustrophobia since my accident. Everyone else wanted to do it, so I decided to just give it a try.

The agent behind the desk smiled at us even before we were all the way inside her office. "Hello," she greeted. "Welcome to Yangshuo."

Kathryn explained what we wanted and the agent set us up with a guide for a tour of the Buddah Caves. The guide explained how we'd crawl through small rock openings. It'd be muddy so "expect to get dirty," but he assured us the mud had healing properties and the caves were breathtaking.

I got nervous. Crawling through a cave was not my idea of fun. *What if I needed to rest?* I was fearful of slipping and hitting my head on a rock. My legs didn't bend easily or painlessly. I was already feeling like there was a metal bar stuck inside my skull, so I changed my mind about the whole thing, turned to my friend, Jenny, and said, "I'm not going."

"Are you kidding, Jennifer? This is a once-in-a-lifetime opportunity. Come on, it'll be awesome!"

Maybe she's right, I thought. And against my better judgment, I agreed to go on the Buddha Cave tour.

The cave was about 50 miles from our hotel in Yangshuo, so we took a long, bumpy taxi ride until we pulled over to rent bicycles, and pedal the rest of the way. Although the air was hazy and everything smelled wet, there was something inspiring about riding bikes in the untouched environment. Everything was the way it should be, without buildings or roads. At least it should have been inspiring, but for me it was just frustrating. We were riding on unleveled dirt roads, and each time I went over a bump, my brain felt like it had to play catch-up when my head moved up and down.

By the time we arrived at the entrance, I wanted nothing more than to collapse on the ground, and lay there forever. Our Chinese guide led us into the cave as he explained its history. I didn't pay attention to anything he said because I was so worried about crawling through rocks. I wondered how often someone had suffocated inside the cave. Jenny and Kathryn looked like they were in high spirits. I couldn't believe they were actually enjoying themselves.

"This end of path ladies," our guide explained. "Now must climb over rock to next side."

Kathryn jumped in front, "Cool! I'll go first."

The rock was only six feet high. The guide held his hands together below his knees, formed a step for Kathryn, and she easily catapulted over. Everyone was able to jump over after bracing themselves on the wall, with a push from the guide; everyone except for me.

When it was my turn, I set my foot on the guide's makeshift launch pad, and he lifted me up. My feet did exactly what they were supposed to and moved up right into my knees, which bent until they hit my chest. I forgot to move my arms up.

"Jennifer, give me your hand," nameless girl ordered. I knew who she was this time, but I couldn't think of her name. It was a stressful situation, so I forgot words. I reached up to let her grab one hand, while another girl grabbed the other. They pulled and the guide pushed. What began as me only caressing the rock became me scraping it with my front side. Again, it felt like a metal bar had shot through my head.

"C'mon Jen, don't be wimpy. You have to push yourself up, it's not that hard," I heard the other girl say (it was Jenny, but I couldn't remember her name).

"I feel so weak and tired, though."

"That's all in your head. Just climb up. We're waiting and this is getting ridiculous."

Our guide pushed my butt up with his backside. It was almost amusing I couldn't get myself up because, after all, it wasn't a massive rock requiring climbing gear or anything. She was right, it wasn't that hard, but I was utterly exhausted, and couldn't tell my body what to do. Eventually the pushing and pulling worked, and I got over the wall.

I was miserable and covered with mud. The guide looked at me, and in broken English said, "You person only like Taxis."

When we returned from Yangshuo, our program director, Chris, wanted our entire teaching group to gather in the vault for a meeting. The vault was a locked room with wall-to-wall cement and without windows. It's the place where all teaching resources, such as games, books, toys, and lesson plans, were kept. But this time it would be the place where we heard the bad news.

"The Guangzhou police are refusing our visas right now," Chris explained. "They don't believe you are really students and think you're getting paid to teach in China without getting permission from the proper authorities. We may be forced to leave the country."

Chris made sure we understood that government officials could be looking around the school asking questions. We were to tell them that we weren't teachers, but students who paid to come to China. It was a cultural experience for us and nothing more. This was the truth, except for the fact that I wasn't really a college student anymore, but no government official needed to know that.

Two days later there was another meeting in the vault. Chris told us the government had agreed to renew our current visas only if we taught conversational English to the Chinese staff at the school. We couldn't teach the children anymore, and we had to attend Mandarin language classes.

"If you don't like the new teaching arrangement," Chris explained, "I'll get you on a flight back to the United States, and you'll be refunded the money you paid for the 2nd half. It's your choice. But, if you do choose to stay, this is a fabulous opportunity to explore China. Plus, you'll have more time to travel. We're going to take a week off from teaching, and hopefully at that point the government will have more details for us, so you can tell me then what you decide."

We'd only been in China for one month and already things were changing. I went to my room and plopped across my bed. *The Chinese government is so bureaucratic. I'm a woman of purpose, and now I don't have one. I am not just going to stick around and do nothing except converse in English with the occasional Chinese person, and go visit tourist sites with 20 year old college students. I'm sick of being tired all the time, so I'm going home to get on with my life.*

I felt good about my decision to return home, and was about to walk to school and tell Chris. But, first I needed to let my parents know. I was certain they'd be happy about seeing me soon. Sitting on the living room couch, I dialed my parent's number and my dad answered.

"Ni hao, Dad!"

"Well. Jennifer! Jennifer Mosher? Is that you?"

My dad does this thing where he always says, "well" before my name, and then pauses as if that one word is its own sentence. Then he'll say my last name like a question, as if he's unsure which of his daughters named Jennifer he was talking to, even though he only has one. It's our little phone game and, as always, I gladly fooled around with him.

"Ah-yeah. It's me. Is this Tom Mosher, my dad?"

This playful sarcasm went on for less than a minute and then he asked me, "So, how's it going Jennifer?"

"It's okay Dad, but this whole thing is not like I expected. The Chinese government is taking away our visas, so we have to stay as students and just teach conversational English to the adults. We can't teach the kids anymore," I explained a mouthful really fast. "It's stupid, Dad. All the other teachers in my group are younger than me, and I feel like I'm wasting my time." I told him we'd been given the option to go home now that our purpose in China had changed. "I've decided to come home. My time in China is over."

At first, I didn't tell him that I'd become uncharacteristically impatient around kids, and about my aversion to large groups. I just talked about my job. "When we were teaching at the school," I explained. "I knew what was expected of me and I worked hard to do it. I'll get too bored if I stay, with nothing to do."

There was definitely more to my decision to leave, and I wanted to be honest with my dad. He might as well know the whole truth. "The other teachers can stay up late and explore the real China. But, all I want to do is sleep and shut my brain off," I confessed. "I feel like I'm in over my head."

Dad's reaction surprised me. "Jennifer, if it were me, I wouldn't even hesitate to stay in China. I mean it is 1997, the year that Hong Kong gets handed back over to the mainland. You'll never have the chance to see that country under the same circumstances."

There was a problem that he wasn't seeing. No one saw it.

"But Dad—," and I stopped for a moment. "It's just so hard for me to feel normal. When we were teaching at the school at least I had purpose and a schedule. Without that, I just have to figure out things to do. I mean, we can travel and explore, but I feel so limited because it's not easy for me to do the things that everyone else does. I still do them, but it's scary."

"Why do you participate in those activities if they're too hard for you?"

"I–I–Dad," and then I got choked up. I felt a tear trickle down my cheek as I thought about my experience at the Buddha Caves in Yangshuo. "I don't like not participating. I try to push through in hopes that it won't be too hard for me, but it always is; everything is always too hard for me."

"I'm a big believer in finishing what you've started, Jennifer. You've taken the road less traveled by even making the choice to go to China. Now it sounds like you have an opportunity to make your experience what you want. This is a once-in-a-lifetime experience, and I don't want you to regret leaving."

Such a typical Tom Mosher response. Dad loved to quote from Robert Frost's poem *The Road Not Taken* any chance he got. I remember him always encouraging me to work hard at everything, especially new activities. Failure was okay in our family, but giving less than our best was not. The problem was that usually I failed at something simply because, as Dad said, I hadn't tried my best. But, now that I was brain injured, I found myself having to work even harder at everything, and I didn't feel like I was succeeding at anything. I was experiencing a whole new kind of failure. I hate failure. I hate letting others down. I hate letting myself down, and if I left China, I knew I'd be doing all three. Dad was right, my experience would be a once-in-a-lifetime opportunity, so I decided to stay and make the best of it.

11

Note to Self: Go North to Beijing

If you never change your mind, why have one?

~Edward de Bono

After four months, a group of us traveled on the Chinese railway system 1,200 miles north to Beijing. The country is packed with people everywhere, and these trains were no different. There are four kinds of train seats in China: soft sleeper, hard sleeper, soft seat and hard seat. Soft sleeper is the superior way to travel as it has a private compartment, and is fitted to a higher standard with upgraded pillows and linens. It's also the most expensive which means that only the most upper-class Chinese travel this way.

Everyone in our group bought hard seats, thinking it was the most authentic way to travel; I splurged and bought a hard sleeper. The hard sleeper is less expensive than the soft sleeper, but not as comfortable. Bedding is basic with an uncomfortable pillow and a rough, scratchy blanket. But, at least I got to lie down and try to sleep. I remember the man in the bunk below mine was chattering loudly in Chinese to the man across from him. I would have given everything to know the Chinese words for "Shut up!" but I didn't, so I just tried to tune him out.

More than anything, I was glad I didn't buy a hard seat like everyone else. Sleep looked impossible for them. You sit on a hard, upright, un-upholstered, uncomfortable seat. It's noisy, crowded, and not very clean. During peak travel times, there tends to be standing room only.

Our train arrived into Beijing at 5:00 A.M. This was distressingly early for everyone, but at least I'd gotten a little sleep. After checking into our hotel, we went directly to Tiananmen Square and squeezed ourselves into a large mass of people behind a roped off area to watch the patriotic changing of the guard. I'm not short, but I had to stand on my tip-toes because the Chinese people in Beijing are much taller than the people in Guangzhou. As I strained to look, a Chinese man tapped me on the shoulder and asked, in perfect English, "Hi, are you from the U.S.A?" It was nice to hear English from someone who didn't look American or European.

"Yeah," I answered. "Are you?"

"My name's Peter. I was born and raised in China, but I live in the U.S. now." He stayed in China through college, but completed graduate school in the United States, and now resided in Los Angeles. "I played volleyball at Northern Iowa University where I got my master's degree," he proudly claimed, until I cut him off.

"I'm from Minnesota!" I announced, as if being from a bordering Midwestern state made for an instant connection between us. That's all I said though, because I slipped back into my spot so I wouldn't lose my place in line, and I could still hear Peter. Besides, I didn't want to concentrate on anything other than my painful, pulsating hips.

He went on to explain he owned a business exporting technical equipment from China. He seemed happy to meet fellow Americans, and promised to show us around Beijing if we needed help, so we exchanged phone numbers.

"I think we're heading over to the Forbidden City now if you want to go with us," I said, after stepping back into the conversation.

Peter paused and stumbled a little. "Thank you," he answered, "but I have other things to do today, and I need to visit my Chinese friends. I'll call you guys later though," he promised.

"Yeah right, like he's going to call us," Kathryn said, as we both watched Peter walk off.

"Well, he said he'd call. Why would he say that if he wasn't going to call?"

"Because he's Chinese, Jennifer! You invited him to go to the Forbidden City with us and since he said 'no,' he has to save face somehow, so he just lied and said 'I'll call you later.' That's totally Chinese."

Maybe Kathryn was right. The whole saving face thing was definitely Chinese, but Peter had lived in America long enough that I just expected him to be past it. "Hmmm, well maybe," I said and we walked to the Forbidden City.

Located north of Tiananmen Square, the enormous Forbidden City is so called because it was off-limits to most of the world for 500 years. Now the public can tour its roughly 720,000 square meters of 800 buildings. We couldn't see the entire city, so we spent the majority of our time in the Palace Museum. Kathryn and I walked around together.

"Kathryn! Check this out!" I screamed loudly as we walked passed a silk scroll depicting a beautiful landscape. "We studied that painting in my Asian Humanities class at BYU," I said, pointing to *Returning Boats on a Snowy River*.

"That's cool you took that class," she calmly responded.

"No, you don't understand. I actually remember reading about that painting! I don't remember very many things." It was a perfect time to tell Kathryn about my brain injury, but I didn't admit anything out loud. *That's not true*, I silently said. *I can remember pretty much everything from before my car accident. I remember running to Spanish class in Chile, with Stacie after we overslept, and I remember dancing at La Oz.* Just then my thoughts were broken up by a man's voice.

"That's one of my favorite pieces from the Song Dynasty. You ladies look like fellow Americans, so I couldn't resist approaching you! Hi, my name's Craig." Smiling, he reached out to give us a formal, business hand-shake. "Oh sorry, the handshake is just habit. I'm still in professional mode. I recently quit my job in San Francisco."

"Our group was in San Francisco before coming to China. We loved Chinatown. There are a lot of similarities between that area and China," Kathryn told him.

"Yeah—that's true, but it's different there because Chinatown is still the United States and it's still democratic. You can feel freedom there. So, do you guys live in California?"

"Well, I'm from Minnesota," I answered, "but most everyone else with us is from Utah."

"Cool, I've been to both Minneapolis and the Salt Lake area. Minneapolis has some great art museums and I'm a skier, so I like Utah for that reason. There's not much else there, as far as I can tell. Are you girls Mormon?"

We nodded, but never had a chance to say anything more about our religion. Craig kept talking. He went on to explain that he'd left a prestigious position at a bank to travel for six months. Before arriving in China, he spent time in Europe. Craig had a sharp perspective, which made me wished I'd had his experiences.

"France is by far my favorite country in Western Europe. It's interesting to experience the differences between the Eastern and Western parts of the world. China is not a different country, it's a different world altogether."

"Definitely!" I agreed. "I've never been to France but it's on my list. I'm dying to see Paris. Yeah, and I totally agree about China being a different world." We spent the next hour absorbed in conversation, as we strolled through the palace.

"Are you ladies hungry? There's this great place around the corner where we can get Peking Duck. Dinner will be my treat."

Kathryn and I followed Craig to the restaurant where we dined on duck, vegetables, and rice. The meal was delectable, and I loved the conversation. Like me, Craig had studied humanities in college, but at Johns Hopkins University, and later went on to law school (which is originally what I wanted to do). He never practiced law, and somehow fell into banking as a career. After describing more about his job—the prestige, the income, and the respect—I grew suspicious of why someone would leave all that behind.

"It took me a while to admit that banking wasn't making me happy," he explained. "The money was great, but I was overworked and burned out. There's so much of the world I want to see, and I'm not getting any younger." He took a bite of duck and changed the subject. "Do you guys know who Edward de Bono is?" It was obvious by our blank stares we didn't.

"Well, he's a leading authority in creative thinking. He actually coined the term 'lateral thinking,' which is the instant perception that blocks the mind's ability to explore alternatives." Then he explained how this related to him. "As for my life, it's like I'd forgotten how to think outside the box. I went to law school, I was a banker. It's what I did—I wasn't happy doing it, but it's what I did. My favorite Edward de Bono quote is 'Unhappiness is best defined as the difference between our talents and our expectations.' My talents weren't meshing with my expectations. Luckily I wised up, quit my job and here I am!"

As Craig was talking, I thought about the expectations I'd developed for my own life. It was easy for someone like him who completed graduate school, had great career, and earned a lot of money to decide what he wanted and just do it. But, things weren't like this for me because I had limits due to my injury. He had no limits. There must have been some other reason why he quit his job.

"Craig," I said. "So, you seriously just quit your job and took off? What if the job wasn't what was making you unhappy? What if it was something else?"

I didn't say anything more out loud, but I thought more to myself: *At least Craig had the option to do what he wanted. At least he doesn't have an uncontrollable, debilitating brain injury making decisions for him. Why did the stupid accident have to happen to me?*

"Jennifer," said Craig. "De Bono also said that you can analyze the past, but you have to design the future. For me, this means that we are in control. You can't expect something or someone other than yourself to make you happy."

I could feel the metal bar stuck in my head. The conversation was giving me a headache. "Yeah, you're probably right," I told him, but I said other things silently: *Probably? I should have said, 'You're partially right' because I feel so different in comparison to you. You wanted to be successful and you are. I want to be successful, but I can't. It's great that people like you can be so idealistic about the future, but what would happen if you injured your brain in a car accident?* My blood started to boil. *What about people like me who can't make it through the day comfortably without two naps? How am I supposed to do what I want to do?* Craig chimed in again.

"Anyway, Jennifer and Kathryn it was great to meet you! I've got to get going." He smiled and set his business card on the table in front of us. "Keep in touch, my email address is on the card. I'm heading to Australia soon, but I'll back in the US after that, so if you guys are ever in San Francisco, let me know!" Our waitress came over to the table. Craig handed her a few Yuan; she nodded, but didn't smile. Craig turned to us, winked, and was off. That was the last we ever saw of him.

Kathryn raised her eyebrows after he left and said, "Hmm, that was weird. You meet the most interesting people traveling! C'mon, let's get back to the hotel."

Two days later, three other girls and I took a taxi fifteen kilometers to the Summer Palace, where Chinese Emperors spent their summers. Well-groomed trees and a lake surrounded the beautiful palace. Everything was so peaceful that I just wanted to sit while the other two girls walked around. I felt like I should go with them because it might be only chance to see the historical site, but every muscle in my body hurt. I felt like one big bruise, so I just found a rock and sat down.

I wondered if I looked as swollen and as purple as I felt. I wondered if people looked at me and thought "How can she even walk?" My head pounded. *No one understands. I feel like my body just went through a torture chamber.*

"Jennifer, are you okay?" my thoughts were interrupted by Jenny. "You're just sitting here alone. Are you sick or something?"

"Um—yeah," I told her, fighting back the tears. "I just hurt really badly."

"Oh yeah, you climbed *The Great Wall* yesterday, didn't you?"

I'd forgotten that I had climbed *The Great Wall of China* with some others in our group. Most of my friends wanted to hike and climb up a completely unrestored part of the wall, but I knew it'd be too much for me, so I convinced them to go to another part instead. It was only partially restored, but completely tourist-infected with people selling all kinds of Chinese trinkets. We walked and walked and climbed and climbed what felt like a million stairs. Once on top, I walked along part of it until I stopped.

"I'll just wait here and watch you guys," I declared, as I sat down on the dirt. I'm sure everyone was tired of my complaining, so they just let me do my thing as they bustled off.

I took off my tennis shoes and looked down at my feet, expecting them to be cut and bruised. But, they didn't look at all like they felt. They looked fine. My entire body felt like a pile of clumpy mashed potatoes.

Earlier, I'd noticed a train taking tourists up and down the wall, but none of my friends were using it, and knew I'd feel like a party-pooper if I used it. But, at that point, I was in so much pain from walking, that I decided to give in and take the train. As I walked towards it, I ran into a Swedish woman and we started talking. "My name is Greta," she introduced herself.

"Hi, I'm Jennifer," I said. I enjoyed meeting other travelers and since I was tired of walking alone, I was happy to talk with her. We walked and talked about how incredible *The Great Wall* was, and how kindly the Chinese people treated foreigners. Our conversation went so long that I missed the point where the train started. Once Greta left, my clumpy mashed potato legs and I had to stumble down those million stairs alone.

Back at the Summer Palace, Jenny was still waiting for me to answer her question. "Yes, I climbed *The Great Wall* yesterday and I'm pretty sore."

"I'm sorry. Is there anything I can do?" Jenny offered. I'm sure she was sincere, but I knew there was nothing she could do other than switch places with me, so I could take a break from living inside my bruised body with an injured brain.

"Oh, thanks but I'll be fine. I'm just going to sit here for a while," I answered. She took that as her cue to leave, and marched down the path away from me.

I wished I didn't hurt so much because it really was breathtaking at the Summer Palace. Then I realized that I was supposed to meet the rest of the group in about one hour to go back to our hotel. An hour was plenty of time, but I knew I was slow, so I started walking to the meeting place. Eventually I met up with my friends and we made it back to our hotel.

I was exhausted when we returned from Beijing a couple days later, and did absolutely nothing for as long possible. I even lied to my roommates and told them I had a fever so they wouldn't ask any questions. I did, however, walk to the computer lab one day, to write Brent an email.

I explained that the Chinese government wouldn't let us teach at the school anymore, and at first I wanted to return home, but I'd reluctantly decided to stay. "This whole thing almost seems like more effort than it's worth," I wrote. After sending the email, I walked to the cafeteria to eat, and then back to my apartment to sleep.

For the next day, all I could think about was how the humid summer air in Panyu was thicker than the humid air in Minnesota. It was even hard to breathe. I was worn out, bored, and didn't know if I'd made the right decision by staying in China. But, once I received a return email from Brent, my perspective changed.

> *Dear Jennifer,*
>
> *I'm really sorry things are so hard for you. At first I was excited for you to come home, but now I'm glad you've decided to stay. The fact that you have this experience is great, no matter how you twist it. I've included a list called "Ten Rules of Happiness." I found it in a magazine, and thought you might like to read it.*
>
> *Love, Brent*

The list had nine predictable rules of happiness. Rules such as "Do your best this hour and you'll do better the next," and "Entertain upbuilding thoughts." The tenth rule was not predictable, and as soon as I read it I felt like I'd been slapped in the face:

Do things which are hard to do.

Brent was one of the few people who understood my injury. He knew I was forgetful and easily exhausted. When Craig quoted Edward de Bono's idea about being in control of our own future, I assumed it didn't apply to me since I couldn't control my brain injury, which controlled my future. Besides, I was sure if Craig had known about my situation, he wouldn't have made the comment in the first place. But, Brent sat with me in the hospital and helped me as I struggled through college. For this reason, I choked up just reading his letter. I read the tenth rule over and over again: *Do things which are hard to do; do things which are hard to do*

I did do things which were hard for me to do, and it irritated me that my hard was not what I wanted to be hard. I wanted my life to be hard as I struggled through a difficult graduate program or because of my responsibility at work. Not because I had trouble climbing over a six foot rock in Yangshuo, China; not because I couldn't remember the first name of someone I'd met a dozen times; not because dancing with my friends late at night was unbearable for me.

At the end of six months, many teachers took a few more weeks to tour to Cambodia, Thailand, and Vietnam. I also wanted to explore those countries, but I was too exhausted to do it. Much of my time traveling was spent figuring out ways to hide my deficits, and I couldn't do this anymore. As much as I enjoyed meeting Peter from L.A, Craig from San Francisco, Greta from Sweden and seeing the sights of China, I ached for American comforts.

Life in China was difficult for me. Not only was I in an unfamiliar country where they spoke a language I didn't understand, but many of the activities I participated in were physically and neurologically challenging. I expected things to become easier after returning home, but I was wrong. Life handed me another pack of experiences where, once again, I needed to confront my life with a Traumatic Brain Injury.

12

Note to Self: Get a Job

Nothing will work unless you do.

~Maya Angelou

When I returned home, I did everything I could to find a suitable job: I searched online, in the newspaper, and even worked with a temporary agency. Once I interviewed for an administrative assistant job at a Minneapolis company that exported educational materials to China. I didn't understand exactly what that meant, but it sounded like the perfect fit for me, since I'd just returned from teaching in China.

I left a little early for the interview because it was the middle of a Minnesota winter and snowing outside. I frantically trudged into the office a few minutes late, covered in white snow flakes.

"Hi…ah…hi, I'm Jennifer Mosher, here for…ah…the interview," I said, winded. The receptionist pointed to a closet where I could hang my coat, as two men dressed in suits entered the lobby.

"Hi Jennifer; thanks for coming. Can we get you any coffee?"

"No thanks," I answered, since I didn't drink coffee. I followed them into a conference room and sat at a large table.

"So Jennifer, I see from your resume that you've just returned from China. That's great! How's your Chinese?" the interviewer asked.

The question surprised me, as I was almost certain that when he called to schedule the interview I'd told him I couldn't speak Chinese.

"Um, well, yeah, I lived in China, but the language is really hard and, um, I don't feel comfortable saying I speak Chinese or whatever. I thought I told you that over the phone." I felt awkward. *Did I really tell him that I couldn't speak Chinese? Maybe he just assumed I could speak, since I lived in China for six months. Could he speak Chinese?* I never knew if I actually said stuff out loud or just thought it.

"Okay, yeah I guess you may have said your Chinese isn't that great, but you must be able to understand something. You were there for six months, right?"

I rattled off the few Chinese phrases I knew; meanwhile hoping he'd ask me about something else. Looking around the room, I saw what appeared to be an old typewriter on a small table in the corner. *Who uses a typewriter anymore?* The white walls were covered with framed posters of educational development awards. Some were even written in Chinese characters.

My mind wandered. *I should have paid more attention during Mandarin class, because then maybe I'd be able to read this stuff. Wŏmen. That's how you say "we." I still know how to say, "We are American," in Chinese because we used to say that all the time. "Wŏmen shì mĕi guó ren."*

I felt so tired. I hadn't slept well the night before, not only because of my sleep disorder, but because I was nervous about the interview. One of the men interrupted my thoughts.

"...so that's what I think, Jennifer. We appreciate you taking the time to meet with us." I don't know how long he'd been talking when I wasn't listening, but I imagine "I don't think you're the right fit for us" was said, so I thanked them and left.

Several months later, a temporary job did turn into something permanent. I worked as an administrative assistant at a financial planning corporation in downtown Minneapolis; nothing related to my college degree. I didn't say anything to anyone at this job about my Traumatic Brain Injury, which meant I felt like I was hiding something. I really liked the work, but every day I had to drag myself there because every day I was worn out.

My duties were basic and boring. More organizing and arranging than figuring and analyzing: data entry, organizing team events, making travel arrangements, and filing documents. I was always pleasant, but not the most efficient employee because my hundredth day at the job felt as unfamiliar as my first. I had the most trouble with filing—a simple office task that should be easy for a hard working, college-graduate with a few years of office experience. But for me, a brain-injured girl with these credentials, filing was like trying to read a book full of nothing but empty pages.

Every month I was to file our client reports. My co-worker, Julie, did show me this task when I first started, but every month I had to remind myself how to do it. One-by-one, a single paper went in each file, categorized in a particular order. I thought this was the process, but I wasn't always sure and usually needed to peek at my cheat sheet.

First was the title page. *Title page. Title page. What does that look like?* My brain moved in slow motion. Eventually I found the title page for the first company: *Alcoa*. There were fifteen more companies, which meant fifteen more title pages. *Next is, um, the title page for, um, um, they're in alphabetical order, right? What did I eat for breakfast again? I don't remember. What did I do last night? I dunno.* I picked up the title page for the next company, and eventually figured out its appropriate place. An hour later, I was still filing.

Although things became a little easier over time, my brain hurt anytime I had to multitask at work. It felt like a pain traveled inside my head with no place to go. Sometimes I couldn't even make sense of things when I was brain injury tired (or, cognitively tired). This is not only a drowsy, I-wish-I-could-close-my-eyelids-for-just-a-short-while-because-they-burn-so-much kind of tired. Brain injury tired hurts more than this. You feel like your head might burst from being overloaded with too much information. This kind of tired is so disabling, that when it happens to me, I can't remember what I need to do to relax or fall asleep.

Back then, every morning when my alarm went off at six thirty, I wondered if someone stood over my bedside while banging two metal pipes together, right into my ear. It was dreadful. I hated my alarm clock, especially if I'd been trying to fall asleep for hours anyway. But, somehow I always got ready in time to catch the city bus to work.

One morning, I saw my bus coming after I'd made it just half-way down the block. Thinking I'd miss it, I started to run. I ran so fast across the street that I didn't even notice my shoes were still untied. Looking down, I miscalculated the time it would take me to step onto the street median, and the back end of my right foot failed to reach the step as my left foot kept moving.

Next thing I knew, I was down on my knees, one shoe on and one shoe off. My wallet and keys had tumbled from my purse, just as I'd tumbled out of my mind, forgetting how to walk. I somehow picked myself up, picked up my things, and limped to the corner just as the bus pulled up.

"You okay?" the driver asked, as I staggered onto the bus.

"Ah...um...yeah, um, I'm fine, I'm totally fine, just kinda embarrassed," I stuttered my response, as both ends of my body pulsated. My head throbbed from a constant spinning, and my ankle throbbed because I'd twisted it in the tumble. *Why didn't I remember to tie my shoes this morning? I'm so dumb.*

Thankfully, there was an elevator in my office building, so I only had to hop a few steps to my cubicle.

"Good morning, Jennifer," I heard my manager's energetic voice call out, as I limped past her.

"Hi, Debbie," I answered and plummeted into my desk chair. I turned on my computer, just as I did every morning, and fumbled around the mess on my desk, just as I did every morning, frantically opened drawers, and searched for my list of daily tasks, just as I did every morning. After working full-time for a few months, I made a reminder list of what I needed to accomplish each day. Before I had this list, the pain in my head felt worse as I struggled to recall my simple tasks:

1. Turn on computer
2. Check email
3. Receive daily accounting data from Luxembourg
4. Key into spreadsheet
5. Send spreadsheet to listed email addresses

These were my duties every day, and every day I couldn't remember what they were. Making a list was such an easy solution, and I don't know how I managed without it. Just then I stared down at my ankle, wondering if the throbbing would ever stop. It looked swollen, so I decided to elevate it on the desk.

"Jennifer? What's up with your foot?" my coworker asked as he walked by.

"Oh, hi Sam. I fell as I ran to the bus this morning."

He came over to my desk, took one look at my ankle and said, "Jennifer we should take you to the hospital! It's swollen, maybe it's broken."

I couldn't believe it. *Broken? It never occurred to me that it could be broken.* Sam ran to Debbie's office to tell her about my possible injury, and she called the corporate office to request a wheelchair. Sam pushed me outside three blocks to the nearest hospital. It was all so procedural; I didn't like being the center of attention for something dumb, like tripping at the bus stop.

Crowds of people on the street rushed by, and some stared at us—an interesting duo: a young woman in a wheelchair, dressed in business attire, with a young man in a suit behind her. But, most people quickly scurried past without time to notice anything unusual.

As Sam rolled me to the hospital, I surprisingly saw my mom marching down the sidewalk towards us. She worked just a few blocks away, and happened to be outside on a break. Her eyes were wide, and I could see a look of terror. She later told me that seeing her daughter in a wheelchair again was like being punched-in-the-gut (her expression), because it brought back so many frightful memories.

"Oh...ah...hi...Mom. I fell this morning, ah, on my way to the bus. Twisted my ankle. This is my co-worker, Sam, and he's just taking me for x-rays. I'll be fine." My terse voice sounded angry, but I was just anxious to get away from all the people. "I'll call you when we're done," I promised. I could tell she wasn't satisfied with my explanation, but still we wheeled off.

At the hospital, the doctor examined my ankle to find it only sprained, not broken. I went home and took the rest of the day off.

Later that evening, I wondered what was in store for me now. Not now that I sprained my ankle, but now that my brain was permanently injured. *What is to become of me? How am I still going to accomplish the things I'm determined to accomplish? Things are only as hard as you let yourself believe that they are. Things are only as hard as you let yourself believe that they are.* Regardless of how many times I chanted these words to myself, I still had doubts. My heart pounded and I was mad. *Why was I so injured in a fluke accident? What did I ever do to deserve such a predicament? It's not fair! Where's the justice?* I felt helpless. *This isn't how my life is supposed to be. I'm just a disaster waiting to happen, all because of a brain injury from a stupid car accident.*

I considered my victories. *Twenty-four hours after the accident, a doctor told my mom I might not make it through the night, but I lived. They wondered if I'd ever walk again, yet I walked two months later. Some thought I'd never return to college, but I graduated from BYU with a bachelor's of arts in 1996. I'll just have to work harder now at everything.*

A master's of English at the University of St. Thomas didn't work for me. I already studied English as an undergraduate, and I didn't want more of the same. *What else could I do, though*? I considered returning to BYU where life was familiar, and do a master's of Art History. At one point, my plan was to work at an art museum with this degree. If I couldn't find a job, maybe I could just start volunteering at a museum. *At least I'd seem smart with a master's degree*, I thought. I even discussed this desire with a college professor who knew about my brain injury.

"It may be too much for you, Jennifer. I don't think your brain could handle it," he advised.

His comment made me mad. How did he know what I could handle? "Oh…um…maybe…um…I'll talk to the disability office," were the only words I could get out. Not only was I shocked that he'd doubt me, but I was sad and wondered if maybe he was right.

13

Note to Self: School Starts at 6 P.M.

You may be disappointed if you fail, but
you are doomed if you don't try.

~Beverly Sills

"Debbie, can I talk to you?" I approached my manager, a few days later, as I gathered enough will-power to confront her with my idea to try graduate school. My company offered a generous tuition reimbursement program, and I was compelled to take advantage of it. Enough time had passed since my master's of English attempt that I decided to push my doubts under the rug, and take another stab. Besides, I knew I'd let myself down if I didn't at least try again.

"Sure," she said. "I've got a meeting in 20 minutes, so now's a good time for me," and I followed her into a conference room.

My heart burned because I was going to confess what I was always too chicken to in the past. *This is my big chance*, I thought. Letting her know about my brain injury would explain so many things. It would explain why something as simple as filing paperwork was so challenging for me. It would explain why I was slow and forgetful. As I walked behind her, I concocted a strategy of what I should say:

I want to try the university here. Graduate school. Nebraska. So tired all the time. I was injured in a car accident. Brain injury. Head injury. Traumatic Brain Injury. Which sounds better? The order is jumbled. I forget what I should say. It needs to sound good. Maybe she won't believe me about the brain injury.

As soon as we sat down, the words came out.

"Debbie, I want to try graduate school. I have a brain injury."

That had sounded better in my head.

"I mean, a few years ago I was injured in a car accident. I fractured my neck and I have a brain injury. I get very tired and sometimes I forget stuff, but I want to try graduate school. The University of St. Thomas has a campus downtown for working adults. Classes are just one night a week, and it doesn't start until six o'clock, so I have a little time to rest after work, and I can just walk there and—and—."

My explanation poured from my mouth. Somehow I made sense to her because she signed the paperwork, and later that week I registered for the master's of Business Communication program at the University of St. Thomas.

As much as I struggled to manage everything, school wiped me out. I tried to simplify my life by preplanning: laying out my clothes for the next day, packing my breakfast and my lunch the night before, getting up at 6:45 each morning, and catching a bus downtown at 7:15 A.M. I ate breakfast, put on my makeup, and took a quick power nap all during the 30 minute bus ride.

I ate lunch at my desk while working, and then went into an empty office, with an eye mask and a timer, to nap again for 30 minutes. On school days, I snuck away from my job at 3:30, walked to campus, which was only a few blocks from work, moved into the library for a third power nap, stopped in the cafeteria to get dinner, and scurried off to class.

I took a gamble by registering for two three-hour classes that semester, assuming I could handle the workload. *Business Writing* met on Mondays and *Marketing Communications* met on Wednesdays. I remember proudly strutting into my first Monday class, pleased to be back in school. Plus, it was only the first day so I wasn't agonizingly exhausted yet. Scanning the classroom, I did a quick evaluation of the other students. There were eight long work tables, divided into two rows, with two students at each table; which meant there were only 16 students. The small class size was perfect for me as too many people, too much noise, and too much commotion meant cognitive overload for me.

I chose to sit in the second to the last table. The front was too close to the professor and he might ask me questions, yet I didn't want to sit in the back because I knew I'd lose focus. I purposely plopped my books onto the table and sighed loudly as if to say, "I just finished a stressful day in Corporate America." A few other students smiled at me with agreement, but most everyone was probably just irritated.

The woman behind me looked familiar. It didn't take long to remember her from my 9th grade in high school. I wanted to clarify my thoughts before the teacher arrived, so I turned and said, "Excuse me, did you go to Breck School? I can't remember your name or anything, but I recognize your face." Breck was the private, college preparatory school I attended during elementary school and junior high until I transferred to the Minneapolis Public High School.

"Yeah! Oh wow!" she answered. "I went to Breck, but that was years ago. Sorry I don't remember you, so I'm surprised you remember me!"

I laughed. "Well, I only went to Breck 1st through 9th grade and—"

"—yeah, I started in 9th grade," she interrupted.

I continued with my story. "The reason I remember you is that you were dating a really cute, super popular football player with dark hair." As I said before, a brain injury hadn't affected my long-term memory.

"Ha!" she laughed. "That cute football player is Brad, and we're married now." Just then an older man with ruffled gray hair, and a perfectly pressed, navy-blue suit walked into the classroom. Obviously, this was the professor, so I smiled at my new friend and turned to face the front.

After welcoming us to class and explaining the course requirements, the professor shared his background. He'd lived as long as he could as a starving fiction writer, but found a sales job when the money ran out. "My supervisor quickly noticed my sales figures were better than average," he said. "But, he also read my appealing and effective client letters, drawing a correlation between the two. Eventually, I began contract writing for hundreds of companies. In addition to college teaching, this has been my career ever since," he explained. "I feel nothing but passion for business writing. Even the shortest document can engage, if it's written crisp and clearly."

I like this man, I silently told myself. *He's clever*. I admired that his career combined the left-brain—analysis and accuracy, with the right-brain—aesthetics and creativity.

"Before we begin, I'd like to know who you are, and how you use business writing in your occupation," he insisted. Then he said something which made me nervous. He wanted all of us to stand and give a brief self-introduction to the class. "State your name, your undergraduate degree, your current job, and why you're in this class."

If he only knew, I thought. *I can't recall even the most basic information when I'm put on the spot.* I felt tired and dizzy. *What's my job, again? What's my name?* I scribbled little notes to myself, so wouldn't forget what to say.

When it was my turn, I stood up and said, "Hi (was I supposed to say "hi" first?), my name is Jennn-nif-er Mooo-sh-er (I knew I had to speak very slowly, or I'd slur my words). I gratu-et-ed from Brig-ham Young Univ-eeers-iteee in hum-an-it-eeees, and I work-for an in-ter-nation-al fin-an-sh-al ad-visor. This is my first class in the prooo-graaam." I quickly sat down, before realizing I'd forgotten to explain how I use business writing in my occupation. Without thinking, I jumped up and blurted out, "Oh, yeah, I read letters at work, um, and sometimes I write notes during class—meetings, I mean I take notes in meetings, not write notes in class!" Everyone chuckled impulsively, even the professor, as if it was the funniest statement they'd ever heard, as if laughter was the medicine they all needed after a long work day. Smiling with everyone else, I sat back down and the next person started.

Somehow I made it through my first day back in graduate school. I fell into my bed as soon as I got home that night.

The next morning, I was still cognitively exhausted after stretching my brain in an academic environment and around new people. This lasted during the next day of work, and through Wednesday's marketing class. Luckily, I still made it to my first class on time. Again, I sat smack dab in the middle.

"Since this class is three hours long, we'll take a ten minute break at 7:30," our marketing professor explained. Silently, I designed a battle plan as to how I'd remain attentive for this and future classes:

1. You don't have to be alert, since it's only the first day.
2. Next week: leave work earlier.
3. Take an hour nap in the library before class begins.

I wrote these strategies in my notes, so I wouldn't forget.

My head felt like it could explode. I squeezed my eyes shut, and tapped my fingers softly on my forehead, which had become a way to still my headaches. This helped only for a little while.

Again, my mind wandered. I looked up and noticed a younger, attractive man at the table next to me. He looked close to my age. *Does he work at a large company like Target or American Express or 3M, or maybe a smaller venture? Is this his first course in the master's of Business Communication program? Did I remember to bring snacks?* I wasn't even hungry, but food gave me an energy boost. I glanced at the woman seated next to me, and then pensively stared out the door into the hallway. Not even paying attention, I felt my neighbor nudge my elbow before passing me a stack of the semester syllabi.

We had one large group project that required a class presentation. The women on either side of me and I agreed to work on ours together. The assignment would be a culmination of everything we'd learn about marketing communications during class. Each group would create a marketing plan for a theoretical vacation club in the Bahamas, and design the overall marketing strategy to implement the brand.

This group project was the most important assignment in the course. I attended all group planning meetings. I took copious notes. I even contemplated our strategy at work, during the time I should have been filing client investment reports. When it was time for us to formulate our presentations, I got together with my group four times in one month; meeting after work, and outside of class. This was too much exertion for my already depleted brain. In fact, I remember feeling complete exhaustion sitting in the student lounge with my group, struggling to keep the large cushy, comfortable chair I sat in from swallowing me up.

One woman took it upon herself to manage our group. "Jennifer, you assemble a list of possible names for the vacation club," she directed, assigning each group member to parts of the plan. In the past, I often volunteered to lead such a group, as I was all about strategy and creating success. But after my injury, I had zero motivation or desire to step up because I doubted if I'd even be able to stand up. So, I just chimed in when I thought I could make sense and hoped for the best.

The professor told us everyone had to speak during our presentation, so I let the self-made group director know that I wanted to speak first. This was all part of my plan. I knew going first meant I'd have to introduce our marketing strategy, but I also knew it meant there would be less time to forget my speech. I could just say my part, and then let myself lose focus because I'd be done, rather than force my already drained brain to struggle through the entire presentation. The other group members jumped at my offer because no one else wanted to be first.

When presentation day came, I felt uneasy, not because I don't like speaking in front of other people, but because I was sure that my words would come out jumbled. *I'll sound stupid. I'll sound like I have no business being in this class and thinking I can handle graduate school. I'll sound unprepared.* I rehearsed in front of the mirror at home, and even practiced with a coworker beforehand. As the first speaker, I knew I needed to capture the audience. I prepared a witty introduction with a joke, and an outline of our presentation, exactly as our professor directed. I took a nap at work. I dressed in appropriate business attire. Everything was prepared.

When my group's turn came, I rose to the occasion. I stepped up in front of everyone, flashed a smile, and told my joke—but no one laughed. Quickly, I turned to my paper, reading what I'd written, and looking up at the audience every so often so as not to sound too monotonous. But, I didn't sound as organized and professional as I did when I practiced in front of the mirror. I remember my speech as mostly "um..." and "ah...so...um," which weren't the words I'd written. After I finished stating our brand and strategy, I passed off to the next presenter. I wished the words "I have a brain injury" were plastered on my face—at least that would explain why I stumbled.

After listening to the other groups, I realized that most everyone stumbled. Many students maintained full time jobs in addition to school, and few were comfortable with public speaking. Everyone said "um" too many times. In comparison, I probably wasn't that bad. But I felt bad. I knew I didn't sound as articulate as I did before my injury because I was different inside.

My brain injury tortured me. What happened to the even-tempered, happy-go-lucky Jennifer? Where did she go? This new person I'd become was often irritable, always drained, and very forgetful. It had been five years since the accident, and I'd spent so much time trying to recover myself that I was bored to tears with it all. Searching for the pre-accident Jennifer was pointless because she was gone forever.

Besides, I was tired of explaining my hidden disability. If asked about my accident, the conversation was always the same:

The question: *What happened?*

The answer: *Car accident. The car rolled in Nebraska. I fractured my neck and both femurs.*

The question: *Were you wearing your seatbelt?*

The answer: *Yes*

The question: *Was it your fault?*

The answer: *No*

The question: *Do you have any permanent injuries?*

The answer: *Yes, I have a Traumatic Brain Injury.*

The question: *You look normal. Do you just get headaches or what does that mean?*

The answer: *Yes, I get headaches, and I also get tired easily. I take multiple naps during the day. I have a bad short-term memory; I forget names and I need to write everything down.*

In an effort to relate and to put me at ease, most people respond with a smile and say, "Oh, maybe I have a brain injury then because I'm terrible with names!" or "I wish I could take more naps," and "I forget what I'm doing all the time" or "You were so lucky."

I am lucky. My life is a miracle. I'm lucky that my family loves me unconditionally. I'm lucky I can reciprocate that love. I'm lucky that the majority of people around me have little awareness of my injury because it means my life is almost back to normal. *Almost.* I will never be completely my old self. I know I'm different—and that awareness hurts. I appreciate the effort to relate, but frankly, whenever people compare general absentmindedness to the forgetfulness that accompanies a Traumatic Brain Injury, it curtails what I've overcome, and I just want to ignore my deficits again.

14

Note to Self: Take Metro to Anvers Stop

A strong positive mental attitude will create more miracles than any wonder drug.

~Patricia Neal

We had some time off between my first and second graduate school semesters, so two friends and I decided to spend a week in France. I've always dreamt of seeing Paris, even back in high school. In fact, I remember sitting in the library with my friend Corinne, listing her French mother's contacts for places to stay if we ever went to Europe.

It had been almost nine years since we made these plans, and I hadn't talked to Corinne since college, so when my friends told me they were planning a trip to France and asked me to join them, I jumped at the chance. The problem was they only wanted to explore the French countryside, and I only wanted to see the city. As a compromise, I checked only myself into a youth hostel in Paris, and the three of us separated for a few days. My journal says it all.

March 19, 1999: I arrived at the youth hostel late last night. I'm anxious to see the many museums and architecture in Paris, everything I learned about in my humanities' classes during college. I feel a bit uneasy about being in a foreign country where I don't know my way around. The only French I speak is the few words I can remember from junior high French class. I have a phrase book, some good walking shoes, and a backpack. I am set for a little mini European vacation, all alone.

When I opened the door to my assigned room at the youth hostel, it was empty. This meant I had my pick of beds. I tossed my backpack next to one of the three bunk beds, and sprawled across it. My eyes felt heavy. I didn't want to fall asleep just yet, so I took a little notebook out of my bag, and planned the day's adventure. Planning for me meant making a very simple list:

4. The Rodin Museum
5. The Sacré-Cœur Basilica
6. The Louvre
7. The Eiffel Tower

These places raced through my mind: Auguste Rodin; *The Mona Lisa* painting; the Eiffel Tower. I wished Corinne was with me since we'd dreamed of visiting Paris together. *High school was so long ago. Why was I even thinking about those days?*

I closed my eyes for a while, hoping to rest. I felt drained and overloaded after a long flight, but I didn't care. I was excited to see the beautiful architecture and art in Paris. The gears in my head turned as I imagined myself on the subway, traveling to the Rodin Museum, a place that looked so beautiful in the pictures. It's a big mansion with grand, arched windows, and magnificent gardens. Not a monstrosity like the Louvre, but a place of character. It was an environment my brain could handle. My dreaming thoughts were broken up when the door opened and two women walked in. "Hello! We're also in this flat," one said in a British accent, both throwing their bags on two empty beds.

"Hi, I'm Jennifer," I answered, still lying in my bed since I was too tired to get up. "Are you guys from England?"

"Yes, London. I'm Callista and this is Rachel. You're American?"

I explained that I was from Minnesota, in the northern part of the United States. We talked a bit more, and then they hurried off to who knows where.

Turning to my list again, I realized I had no idea how to get to The Rodin Museum, and studied the directions in my travel guide: *Take RER C Yellow to Invalides station, take blue 13 to Chatillon-Montrouge. Get off on Varenne? You might just have to walk from Invalides because not sure if Metro stops at Varenne.* I jotted the directions in my notes, put on my tennis shoes, and left the hostel.

Once I arrived at the Metro, my scribbled notes made absolutely no sense to me. I couldn't read my own writing, and I'd written a bunch of arrows, pointing to other illegible words. Eventually, I made it to the museum alone by taking three Metro transfers, reading multiple French street signs, and figuring out my location on the map. It's true what they say, "All you really need to find your way around Paris is a pair of good walking shoes and a good map."

After strolling through the small museum, I felt like my eyes were sinking into my brain again. *Why can't I feel normal, just this once?* I asked myself. *I'm at a museum, in Paris. This is the moment I've dreamed about, but I can't enjoy it.* My eyes weren't tired, but my brain was exhausted; I needed sleep. I walked outside and saw an empty park bench where I knew I could rest. Even on vacation, I had to plan rest breaks around sightseeing.

I sprawled across the park bench, but I don't know how long I rested because, not more than a few minutes later, I heard a French man talking to me, so I sat up. "So mutch valking in Parees vill tire yer legs," he said, flashing a large smile. He stood so close when he talked, I could feel his breath. I couldn't help but smile because his accent was so charming. He was just the energy boost I needed. *French flirting, this is fun.* I asked him for directions to the Sacré-Cœur, even though I had them already written down. He told me to take the Metro to the Anvers stop, which is what it said in my notes.

"Merci," I thanked him in French, trying to flash the same large smile that he gave me, and I was off to the Sacré-Cœur on the Metro.

When I exited the Metro at the Anvers stop, I saw clusters of buildings and people, but I couldn't find the Basilica, so I gazed around, counting six chocolate vendors. The sweet smell was potent. Turning to the first vendor behind me, I bought some chocolate, and *voila*, there was the never-ending flight of stairs leading to a white Basilica with a three-tiered dome on top. I remembered that everyone told me it was a steep hike up the steps to the Sacré-Cœur, so I knew I'd found it. I don't know how I'd missed the stark massive building. The many other structures around must have kept me from paying attention. I expected an hour trek of stairs, but there were only three or four flights of roughly twelve steps each.

Slowly climbing up, taking rest breaks every few steps, I made it to the top, and turned around to see a breathtaking view of Paris. I looked across the tips of a never-ending array of buildings in front of me. Each structure was architecturally magnificent, yet unique. I saw the real version of what I'd only seen in textbooks. The white rooftops were positioned perfectly against a clear, blue sky, like a canvas. It was beautiful. Then I looked down to see the many steps I had climbed to reach the top. The hike felt steeper than it looked.

A man and woman were kissing; another couple was hugging to my right. A few teenage girls were seated in a circle way down on the first set of steps, talking and laughing with each other. I was happy to be there, but I expected to feel differently my first time in Paris. I wished my head didn't feel so heavy, and I wished my thighs weren't pulsating.

Still staring at the view, I sat down on the top step, just before the Basilica, deeply inhaled, and rubbed the knots out of my legs. The colors were striking. Everything in front of me was beautiful, and worth the painful climb.

After the stunning Sacré-Cœur, I roamed the streets of Paris until a man approached and asked to draw a picture of me. "If you like, I make you good price." Normally, he said he charges 300 franc but for me, "because you are so bewt-ee-ful, I do it for 150 franc."

He draws, we talk, he tells me he's not a business man and he does this just for the art. When he'd finished, I told him that 150 franc is about $25, and I didn't really want to buy a cartoon drawing of myself for that price.

He laughed and said, "100 franc, then." $17 is not bad, and I took it. At least I'd have the memory of a charming French artist and his cartoon sketch. I wrote down directions to the youth hostel, so I could make it back and rest. My head spun fast, but the pain was worth the fun I had in Paris that day.

I must have fallen asleep as soon as I crawled in my bunk at the hostel later, because I woke up startled when my alarm went off, feeling like I was Rip Van Winkle in a complete daze. My head shot up, confused about where I was, thinking I'd missed something important, and I grabbed my backpack, ready, to run outside. Luckily, I saw Rachel lying in her bed so I stopped and became oriented to where I was: a youth hostel in Paris.

I returned home one week later, feeling rejuvenated and optimistic about life. I wanted to see and experience more of the world, but it was back to reality and back to Corporate America. Luckily, I could extend my vacation and stay home for two more days to recover from jetlag. My manager Debbie was the first person I saw as soon as I walked back into work.

15

Note to Self: Call Brain Injury Association

He who is afraid of asking is ashamed of learning.

~Danish Proverb

"Jennifer," Debbie said. "We need to talk for a few minutes."

"Okay," I agreed, following her around the corner, into her office. I didn't know why she wanted to talk, but I considered every possible scenario: *I bet I forgot to call a client back, and she received a complaint? She wants to tell me I'm too slow at filing. It's all because of my injury. I've hid it from everyone, and finally Debbie sees through me. I know I'm forgetful, and I ask the same questions over and over about how to do the same things that I've been doing for months. I know I seem stupid. Will I be fired because of this tortuous brain injury? This job wears me down anyway.*

Debbie sat behind her desk, and right away she starting talking, "How are you doing today, Jennifer?"

I smiled. *Fine. I am fine. Stop the small talk.* My pleading was silent.

"Well…Jennifer…as you're aware, ah…there…have been some cutbacks at the company, and unfortunately your position was eliminated. So, I need to lay you off. Currently, there are two people doing your job and now there will be only one. Here is your unemployment compensation information, which will begin in six weeks," she said, handing me a large packet. "I'm really, really sorry."

I was shocked and my face went blank. Debbie probably expected me to burst into tears, but really I wanted to let out an enormous sigh of relief. Her words were like music to my ears. *I was laid off, not fired? I get an unemployment package?*

"Jennifer, if you'd like to take the rest of the day off, that's fine. I can just tell everyone about the lay off when you're not around, if that would make you feel more comfortable."

As much as I appreciated her concern, I didn't feel the least bit uncomfortable, and immediately I told Debbie exactly what I was thinking. "Oh-no, no you can tell everyone right now. I'd prefer to be there because otherwise everyone will walk on eggshells around me, wondering how they should treat me, and what they should say next time I'm at work. Don't worry, Debbie. I'll be okay."

A few minutes later, my entire department gathered around a file cabinet, and Debbie told them. Everyone looked at me, waiting for my reaction. But I was calm, and almost grinning, because soon I'd no longer need to mask my brain injury while struggling through menial office tasks.

My stint in Corporate America ended six weeks later. I decided to finish my current graduate class at the university, and figure out my next move. It would be the perfect opportunity for a career change.

After my injury, I constantly battled between what I wanted to do and what I knew I could successfully do. *I want to move away. But, it takes me a ridiculously long time to feel comfortable in new places* (I always get lost*). I want a graduate degree. But, I can't remember what I read in textbook, or pay attention in class.* Yet again, I was tired of modifying my dreams, all because of the brain injury, all because of a car accident, which was all because I was in the wrong place at the wrong time.

British Statesman, Benjamin Disraeli, once said that action may not always bring happiness, but there is no happiness without action. More than I hate modifying my dreams and changing my goals, do I hate deleting my dreams and not having goals. I needed something new to strive for after my job layoff, something new to do. I considered my options.

The University of St. Thomas had a post-baccalaureate program for prospective teachers to get licensed. I liked teaching and I liked children. Besides, I already had elementary school experience in China (unrealistically assuming my struggle with impatience was only because it was a foreign country, not because of my brain injury). I knew if I were going to pursue graduate school a third time, I needed help, and just where to get it: The Brain Injury Association of America.

Although located in McLean, Virginia, The Brain Injury Association has more than 40 state affiliates across the country, so I was positive there was one in Minnesota. I grabbed the portable telephone lying on my bed. *Where do I keep the phone book? I need to find the phone number.* I plopped down on the floor in my bedroom. *Where's the phone book? Does the Brain Injury Association have a website? I could just look them up on the internet. Too many steps. Must find the phone book.*

My thoughts raced. *Settle down Jennifer! Relax!* I hated when I felt this way, filled with anxiety so I couldn't remember basic information. Often if I just relaxed, took a deep breath, and waited patiently, an idea would wiggle itself around my confused brain and somehow squirm into a place noticeable to me.

Suddenly, I remembered. My phone book was in the middle drawer next to the stove. I scurried into the kitchen only to smell something burning. I quickly scanned for clues about where the odor came from, and I saw scorched bread poking from the toaster. *Oops! I forgot I made toast this morning.* An opened cereal box sat next to the toaster, and I remembered I ate cereal for breakfast. I pulled the cold bread from the toaster. "Yuck," I mumbled, throwing it in the garbage with one hand, and grabbing the phone book with the other to look up the number.

Once I found it, I dialed and a woman answered, "Brain Injury Association of Minnesota—can I help you?"

"Um, yes, hi. I'm looking for...oh, my name is Jennifer Mosher and I have a Traumatic Brain Injury...I mean, I'm a...a...um...brain injury survivor," I explained my status.

"Great! I'm glad you called." I got a little choked up because I knew I was talking to someone who immediately understood me. I paused and swallowed before finishing my answer.

"I need help," I told her, surprised at how easily these words rolled off my tongue. I've since learned that knowing when to ask for help is important to the healing process. I explained to the woman that I'd enrolled in a graduate program while also working full-time, and the workload was almost unbearable for me. "I was recently laid off from my job and I think this is a perfect time for a career change. I'm thinking about elementary education," I explained.

"Now do you think the multitasking around so many little kids would be too much for your brain to handle?" she wisely inquired.

I was surprised, if not appalled, by the question. Obviously she didn't understand how much I could handle. I purposely smiled so I'd sound more pleasant.

"Oh no, I can definitely handle it. I successfully graduated from college. I mean, I'm a good student. I just need help," I explained. "Like untimed tests. I had this in college after my injury, and I need an updated neuropsychological assessment because it's been over five years since my last one. I think I can handle it. I can handle most things. I just don't know where to get the evaluation."

She recommended I call Doctor Thomas Misukanis, a clinical neuropsychologist in private practice. Talking to a neuropsychologist on the phone as a brain injury survivor is like walking naked through a crowd of people—exposed. When I called him, he asked simple questions like my name, phone number, and date of the car accident, but I had trouble remembering the answers. *He can see my brain injury through the phone cord.* I felt awkward, nervous, and embarrassed, but I still set up an appointment to meet with him on December 3, 2002.

16

Note to Self: Your Cover is Blown

Memory is often less about the truth than about what we want it to be.

~David Halberstam

Soon I would meet with a doctor who could blow my cover. I'd manipulated my way through China, through a full-time job, and through a few graduate school classes. But, I knew couldn't manipulate my way through this appointment. I even had trouble getting there.

Dr. Misukanis gave me detailed directions to his office, and I thought I understood where to go. But arriving was a different story. Even though I drove only a few miles, I was so directionally challenged that I might as well have been in a foreign country. For help, I glanced at the scribbled notes I took during our phone conversation. *Go up the stairs*, I read. *Which stairs? The front of the building or the back or the side? His name is not even on this building.* I felt so tired. *Where did he say I should park again?*

When I finally figured out where to go, I felt as if I'd just made it through a maze. Really, I'd only parked the car and climbed one flight of stairs to a metal door that said, "Dr. Thomas Misukanis, clinical neuropsychologist."

I knocked and a tall man with disheveled, sandy-blond hair opened the door, smiling. "You must be Jennifer?" he asked. "Good to see you! Come inside and sit down." He actually spoke with a warm, sincere tone as if he was glad to see me, but I didn't act the same way in return. I was tired and still irritated that I had so much trouble finding his building.

This doctor would probably be considered good-looking if he'd just tuck in his shirt and wear a belt that actually fit his waistline, I thought. I imagined helping him pick out some trendier, smaller eyeglasses to replace the over-sized plastic frames he kept pushing up his nose. I liked helping people with their fashion selections.

Once I even worked for an optometrist in the same office where I did therapy to help my double vision. That job only lasted for one month though. I quit because I struggled to remember what was what and how I was supposed to do everything.

Jean, the office manager for the optometrist, had a photographic memory. She'd always remember every customer's name as soon as they walked in, and would direct them to the exact location of the frames they wore during their last visit. She was incredible. But I felt so exhausted just sitting behind the receptionist desk that I watched the clock until the day was over. One time I did help a man select his eyeglasses, but only because Jean told me to.

Back to Dr. Misukanis: I don't think I said anything directly to him about his out-of-date glasses—but I'm not sure because I tended to say things out loud that began as just a thought. It's like I had a courtesy filter missing or something. Plus, I forgot things all the time, like where I'd put my own glasses when they sat on top of my head. I often wondered what I did with my keys when they were on the kitchen counter, where I always put them. I knew I'd eaten breakfast in the morning, but only because I didn't feel hunger pains, not because I remembered putting something in my mouth.

"Jennifer? Jennifer?" Dr. Misukanis said my name twice to pull me out of my dreams.

"Oh…ah…yeah?"

"First I'd like to make sure I understand your situation and background, and then I'll administer some neuropsychological exams that test your I.Q, your verbal fluency, and memory. You may recognize these tests because you probably also took them in the hospital. Give me one week and I'll mail you an evaluation."

I perked up. If I'd done these tests before, then there was a chance I'd remember them and could slip by better. "I think I'll do fine," I explained, feeling like I had to defend myself. "I mean, I was badly injured, but that was a long time ago. Now I'm way better. I'm a college graduate, working full time and stuff."

"Alright, Jennifer, I'm sure you'll do the best you can," he assured me. "So, the reason you contacted me for this evaluation is because you'd like to go back to graduate school, right?"

"Yeah, and because I need untimed tests," I interrupted. "I mean, I need documentation proving I'm brain injured so I can get the proper accommodations at school."

"Right; and you've already taken graduate classes. How did that work for you?"

"Oh, well…um…it was tough. I worked full time and these classes were three hours long at night. I was just so exhausted. I loved the classes, but was pretty worn out after work, so it was hard to pay attention in class."

Dr. Misukanis scribbled something in his notes, while nodding his head. "Okay, we'll take a lunch break at noon. There are some vending machines downstairs if you forgot to bring anything to eat."

"No, I brought food," I responded curtly, probably because I was so nervous. I always feel nervous when I talk about my brain injury. My eyes tingled and my head burned. I looked down at my book bag on the floor and wondered if I'd put any cheese or mayo on my sandwich. *Those things spoil when they're not refrigerated, right? I hate warm cheese. If only I could curl up on the floor for a few minutes, I'd be a different person. I'm so tired.*

"Jennifer, let's get started with the first test, okay? You'll probably recognize this one."

Just like my testing with Dr. Morgan at The Minneapolis Clinic of Neurology, I was placed in front of a foam board full of holes cut into various shapes. I had to place corresponding shaped blocks into the holes while blindfolded. Again, I had to redraw the location of the blocks from memory, and again I struggled.

"I need a piece of paper and a pen so I can take notes," I explained, before we started.

"Jennifer, taking notes to compensate for your short term memory loss is a great strategy, but for the validity of these tests, I'm not going to let you do that," he said, which really irritated me.

I can't take any notes? Is he trying to outright humiliate me? I thought this guy was on my side. I thought he understood the struggle of a Traumatic Brain Injury Survivor. Why had he turned against me?

After a few other tests, he wanted to discuss how brain injury affected my personal life. He asked questions such as, "Do you misplace your keys a lot?" and "Do you have trouble sleeping on a regular basis?" and "How is your love life?"

I was offended by the last question. *Why did he even ask about my love life? What does that have to do with my memory and verbal fluency?*

"My love life is fine," I answered. But *none of your business* is what I felt like saying.

"Well, on the average, TBI Survivors have a difficult time maintaining relationships, so that's why I asked the question."

The truth is that I hadn't had a real relationship since before my accident. I never was an *I always need a boyfriend* type of girl anyway, and I didn't really like putting myself in vulnerable emotional positions with men.

I felt uncomfortable talking with Dr. Misukanis about this. For the first time, I wondered if my brain injury had not only affected my memory, sleep, and balance, but also my ability to maintain a relationship, something that was already hard for me.

Glaring at the doctor, I stuck to my story, "Yeah, I don't have much of a problem." That's what I said out loud at least, but the voice inside my head spoke the real truth.

Who'd want to be with me anyway? I'm listless and I don't participate in activities that challenge my balance or memory, especially if I know I can't get a nap afterwards. Why would anyone want to spend time with someone so difficult? I'm tired all the time and sleep doesn't seem to rejuvenate me so I eat to gather more energy. I feel fat.

Dr. Misukanis and I separated for lunch, so he could summarize the tests. I went to the office lunchroom and pulled out my sandwich. The small room was filled with three large round tables and at least three people sat at each table. There were two empty seats, but it wasn't like I'd go up to one of them and ask, "Okay if I sit here?" What if these people were neuropsychologists like Dr. Misukanis?

"I've never seen you before, what are you doing here?" I imagined one of them asking me.

"I'm testing with Dr. Misukanis," I'd say. The cat would be out of the bag, and I'd have to explain why I needed the testing. Then I'd tell them that I wanted to go back to graduate school and either they'd give me that *are you out of your mind* look or an insincere smile and congratulate me for trying so hard.

I was exhausted from talking about my brain injury, so I decided to just sit on the floor against the wall, eat my sandwich, and close my eyes.

After a while, Dr. Misukanis came into the lunchroom to get me. I felt a little better after the short rest, at least well enough to smile when he asked, "How was lunch?" I followed him back up to his office for a few more tests.

At the end of the day, we discussed the tests results, and Dr. Misukanis told me exactly what I didn't want to hear. The first thing he said was "Jennifer, *clearly* you have a brain injury." He told me not to be in class for more than one hour, which explained why the three hour class period after work was so difficult for me.

"It might be time for you to reset your expectations for yourself."

I was surprised. I wanted him to tell me that I'd have absolutely no problem going back to school if I worked hard enough. I thought I could fool him into thinking that my injury was just mild and I had it beat. But, if Dr. Misukanis told me that I clearly had a brain injury, then I had a hard time convincing myself I was okay. In retrospect, I think I was only trying to keep myself fooled. My self-identity was at serious risk. Maybe he was right; maybe I did need to reset my expectations.

Still undeterred from my dreams, the next day I called my sister-in-law, Kimberly, and told her that I thought getting laid off from my job was a good thing because now I could switch careers and do something more meaningful. "I'm thinking about trying to teach elementary education," I said. "They have this great program at the university here called a post-baccalaureate degree. It's more than a bachelor's, but less than a master's."

"I think it sounds great, Jennifer," Kimberly agreed. "You'd be really good. Maybe you should consider a school out in Salt Lake City. It'd be a new environment, but still familiar since you've already lived in Utah while you were at BYU."

Move back to Utah for school? This had never occurred to me but I liked the idea. I decided to set aside my current plan and research schools in Utah. A few days later, I received the test results back from Dr. Misukanis:

> *The present test findings reveal significant cognitive deficits which are most apparent in*

processing speed, initial learning, and short-term memory. Difficulties are also noted in complex or novel problem-solving and verbal fluency. These areas of impairment are clearly the residuals of the severe brain injury.

Deficits. Difficulties. Impairment. Injury. I read these four words as if they were printed in blood red. By simply ignoring my challenges, I thought I had beaten my injury. I thought my life would change only if I let it. However, after reading these results, I realized that maybe I wasn't doing such a good job at hiding my injury. Dr. Misukanis' words, "Clearly you have a brain injury," rang in my head.

I lay on my bed thinking about my life. On one hand, I felt grateful because I was given a wonderful gift, a second chance after surviving a terrible car accident. Initially given the lowest possible score on the Glasgow Coma Scale and not expected to make it through the night, now I was a college graduate with friends and family who loved me, living a full life.

On the other hand, I felt angry and frustrated because I was permanently impaired, and my future was forever changed. I was in my twenties, feeling like I was living inside an eighty year old body. Maybe more school was just a waste. *Was I being unrealistic?* The injuries that the human eye could see, my broken femurs and fractured neck, were fixed but the most traumatic injury, the one inside my brain, was permanent. My head hurt just thinking about this.

As I lay in my bed, I realized that by nurturing these depressing thoughts, I was letting my injury get the best of me. It was like some evil, hungry monster had been set free and was eating away inside my heart. Somehow my anger and frustration unleashed my personal determination not to let this happen. Regardless of the impairments Dr. Misukanis revealed during his cognitive testing, I decided to proceed with my plans to create a new life in Utah.

17

Note to Self: Airplane Leaves Monday

> In three words I can sum up everything I've
> learned about life: it goes on.
>
> ~Robert Frost

I chose to apply to The University of Utah, a large public
university, and Westminster College, a small private college in
Salt Lake City. Graduate school was a perfectly legitimate reason
to move to Utah, but I needed to be sensible too. Although I was
accepted to both schools, just thinking about trying to navigate
myself around a large university gave me a headache, so I put
more effort into learning about Westminster College and their
master's of Education degree.

Arriving in Utah this time was easy. I ran into an old
friend who needed a roommate and we found an apartment. I
made a few friends and *voila* my life was set. Since I was new to
Salt Lake City, I expected to have trouble finding my way around
town, and to have trouble remembering new names. I never even
felt the need to mask my brain injury from anyone during the first
few weeks.

I spent each day job hunting on the internet and calling temporary employment agencies. I attended several meetings with college professors and with the master's of Education Program Coordinator, in hopes they'd help make graduate school more manageable for me. Truthfully, at that point I didn't feel as excited about starting school again, but I also hated changing my mind about big decisions, so I went forward with my plan.

At one meeting, I did own up to my brain injury, and the program coordinator suggested I sit through one evening class to see if I could handle it. Assuming it would be no problem, I selected a course to attend, and she showed me exactly where it met by walking me to the room.

Going on my own the next day was a different story. It wasn't a complicated march, but a Traumatic Brain Injury complicates everything. The class met during the late afternoon, a time when I already feel fatigued, and I was in an unfamiliar environment. The two together put immense strain on my injured brain. I remember standing alone in the middle of campus looking around at all the unfamiliar buildings and having no idea what I was doing. *Where am I going? Why am I here?*

I managed to maneuver my way around and find the classroom. Really, it was just between two buildings and down one flight of stairs. It sounds simple, but just like my travel to The Minneapolis Clinic of Neurology to meet Dr. Morgan, it felt like a tangled cobweb.

Class details were a blur and I had zero desire to listen. I do remember the instructor asking us to apply a chapter in the textbook to a real teaching moment. She sounded interesting, but I barely paid attention because one thought consumed me: *What am I doing here?* I wanted nothing more than to be alone, asleep, or at least resting in my bed without any noise. *My head is pounding. It took so much brain power to find this place. I'm exhausted. I just want to go home. I can't do this.*

And then it hit me. If I was back in school, once again I'd have to explain the brain injury to my professors; I'd have to get more time on tests; I'd have to take a light class load, and classroom teaching meant I'd have to be around a lot of noise and a lot of people (kids) at one time, which brought me to cognitive overload. I didn't know what my next move would be, but I knew what I didn't want. I left class that night with drooping, tired eyes and a smile on my face.

The Jennifer who walked out of Westminster College that night was different than the Jennifer who walked out of The University of St. Thomas a year before. In Minneapolis, I'd ignored my limitations and in Salt Lake I was able to recognize them. The tangled cobweb I felt when I arrived in class must have blown away because I walked directly to my car without a struggle.

It was like an alarm went off inside my head. By continually doing the things which were painfully hard for me (like graduate school), these limitations became confining. I felt like I couldn't be successful at anything. But once I recognized my limits as obvious indicators of what I needed to eliminate, life with a brain injury became easier and I could feel in control again. For the first time in a decade, the words "I have a brain injury" didn't feel so disabling.

I postponed graduate school, again, to focus my energy on something else: healing. I started attending a support group for people with brain injury, and I tried sleeping more. In Minnesota I worked full-time, attended graduate school two nights per week, and tried to live an active social life, all at the same time. Ultimately, I was happy about everything I was doing, but I wasn't happy doing it. I decided to work less and play more in my new Utah life.

Working less was easy. Playing more was not. One day I went to a water park with Kimberly, her sisters and their kids. After hours in the sun and in the pool, surrounded by tons of people, my head spun. Whenever this happened, I had a difficult time talking and making appropriate decisions. The feeling was similar to the day I ran so fast across the street to catch my bus for work, and didn't notice my shoes were untied.

Cognitively exhausted, I returned to a small wading pool in the park. Rather than go down the little slide into the pool, I just stood at the edge, watching at all the young children playing in the water. I didn't want to get wet again, so I decided to walk down the slide, since it was only about five feet long and six feet wide. I took one step, lost my balance, and both my legs flew out from under me. I heard a loud thud, as my butt hit the pavement under the water.

My next clear memory is of me standing in line with Kimberly at the emergency room. "Jennifer has a history of head injury," she told the receptionist.

A while later, still in my bathing suit, I lay on what looked like a white operating table and a doctor asked me, "How are you feeling?"

"I feel strange," I responded. "Like my head is not all there. What happened to me?"

"You fell at the water park," the doctor explained. "There was no blood or physical injury, but the jarring from the fall gave you a minor concussion."

I was confused. I remembered walking to the car and driving to the hospital. "You never lost consciousness," the doctor went on, "but you are far more susceptible to head injury since your car accident."

I stayed at my brother's house that night so he could make sure I remained stable for 24 hours. When my sweet, five-year-old twin nieces, Rachel and Lauren, saw me, they smiled wide enough to show their identical toddler teeth. Each gave me a big hug, and that's when Rachel pointed to the long curved scar above my eyebrows—one of the many scars remaining from my car accident—and said, "Aunt Jennifer, you have a smile on your forehead!"

18

Note to Self: Follow Shelley to Conference

Sleep is the best meditation.

~Dalai Lama

Do you know about the brain injury conference happening in October?" my roommate Shelley asked.

"What?! There's a brain injury conference coming up?" I'm always enthusiastic about attending a conference on any subject, and listening to expert opinions about nearly anything. I also love seeing a good plan put into action. How do they pick the speakers? How is it advertised? Who will prepare the food? How will they register conference attendees? These processes fascinate me.

At the same time, I wondered what made Shelley think I knew about the conference. Was this something she'd mentioned to me before and I just forgot?

Shelley and I didn't know each other before she moved in, but I wanted a roommate to help with expenses, and she responded to an ad I placed. When she came over to look at my condo for the first time, I asked what she did for a living; from her response, I knew she was a good fit for me.

"I'm a social worker," she answered, "working specifically with people with disabilities." She rattled off a few types of disabilities, but I remember only one: Survivors of Traumatic Brain Injury.

"No way! I have a brain injury!" I screamed with the energy of a long lost soul sister. "Yeah, I fractured my neck in a car accident on my way to BYU. I was in a coma ..."

I proceeded to tell her that I needed to sleep a lot, and my short-term memory was terrible. I let her know my job was part-time because I got overloaded with too much stressful information. After only a few words of trying to explain the lingering effects of my brain injury, I realized no explanation was necessary. Shelley understood.

Come October, we walked into the Davis Conference Center in Layton, Utah for The Brain Injury Association of Utah Family and Professionals Conference. There were so many people in attendance that cars had to squish together in the parking lot, like sardines. Since Shelley was with me, I didn't bother taking the time to draw a small map, detailing where we'd parked the car and the location of the exit door. She could remember this information.

Shelley and I went up to a woman sitting behind the check-in table near the entrance.

"Are you a survivor, caregiver, or professional?" she asked.

"Professional," Shelley confirmed her status.

"I'm a survivor!" I declared, proudly. Those three words sounded more important to me at that moment than they ever had before.

The woman gave us each a thick book listing the speakers, session locations and times, as well as some interesting facts about brain injuries. Ernest Hemmingway, I learned, suffered from a diagnosed depressive disorder and alcoholism. Less well known was the fact that he had at least five head injuries during his lifetime. It's thought that his difficulty writing, excessive drinking, depression and even his ultimate suicide were probably the result of his brain injuries. If only Ernest Hemingway had known about his injury and understood how to manage it, maybe he wouldn't have taken his own life.

Each day of the conference had a choice of different session topics. Day one was my favorite because Dr. Mark Ashley[3] spoke on "Cognitive and Physical Fatigue after TBI." I've read many books written by TBI Survivors and talked to many doctors and educators, in search for ways to cope with a Traumatic Brain Injury. Although it's helpful to talk with anyone who understands the residual effects of a TBI, no one has ever been able to help me manage these effects like Dr. Ashley.

All brain injury survivors have cognitive deficits, specifically memory problems. We forget constantly. Embarrassing as this is sometimes, memory loss can be compensated for by making a few adjustments. As I've mentioned, with the help of the disability office, I was given extra time on exams during college. Even now, I keep a calendar, reviewing my schedule multiple times per day. Sometimes I even write down what I've said to people to help prevent asking the same thing to the same person.

For me, however, the hardest part about living with a Traumatic Brain Injury is not the memory loss, it's the sleep disorder. After the accident, I never slept more than four or five hours at one time. It was miserable. I went to bed dead tired, yet it took me two hours to fall asleep, and then I woke up after four hours, still dead tired, and couldn't fall back asleep. This made for an abnormal lifestyle because, like an infant, I always had to take at least two naps during the day. At the lecture, Dr. Ashley told us we should be sleeping seven to nine hours per night,

---

[3] Dr. Mark Ashley is co-founder, president and CEO of the Centre for Neuro Skills, which operates post-acute brain injury rehabilitation programs at facilities in California and Texas.

uninterrupted. I couldn't remember the last time I'd slept even five hours uninterrupted.

His recommendations were simple. In order to control the sleep disorder, we needed to make a few basic lifestyle changes, along with using a prescribed sleep medication. In the entire time since my accident, I hadn't taken any medication (aside from what I took while in the hospital), other than over-the-counter sleeping pills; these made me feel more tired, but didn't help me stay asleep.

After the conference, I was hungry for a good night's sleep, and eager to make changes to my lifestyle to see if they'd help. Dr. Ashley recommended trying a "Southbeach-ish Diet" (his words) by limiting refined carbohydrates and avoiding sugar and salt, especially late in the evening. "Strive for stable levels of glucose in your system and starches convert to glucose quickly," he explained.

"Watch your sodium intake at dinner because too much sodium will make you thirsty, which means you'll drink more liquid. As a result, you'll need to use the restroom in the middle of the night. If you get up to empty your bladder, your biological clock is set for this and will naturally stick to its schedule," he cautioned.

He suggested we prepare for sleep by avoiding exercise in the evenings (but get 20-30 minutes of cardio exercise every other day because regular exercise makes it easier to fall asleep and to stay asleep), avoid alcohol and caffeine, along with other liquids in the evening.

"Do not open your eyes or look at the clock during the night," he said, which is something I'm guilty of. Without fail, I wake up several times in the middle of the night to use the bathroom. After the conference, I just kept my eyes closed as I maneuvered my way to the toilet, then back into bed. Usually I then had an easier time falling back to sleep. My bathroom is only three steps from my bed, however, so this is not unsafe; although I probably looked funny. Admittedly, sometimes I squinted, so as to never bump into anything.

Many TBI Survivors have vestibular problems after their injury, and closing their eyes while walking around, or even walking in low light conditions, could be disastrous. Fortunately, I don't struggle with this very often anymore. For several years after my accident, I wondered if I was going to slip and kill myself every time I walked down a flight of stairs because not only did I feel dizzy, but by multitasking my senses (looking down the staircase, while hanging onto the railing, and concentrating on each step), I became physically unbalanced.

Lastly, Dr. Ashley told us to get to bed at exactly the same time every night to regulate our bedtime clock. "You must be militant about all of this," he advised. It became clear that if I implemented these techniques, I may be able to control at least one effect of my brain injury.

For the next week, I exercised at the gym in the morning and didn't eat sugar or sodium in the evening. I didn't open my eyes or look at the clock if I did wake up. The change was almost immediate. I think I slept nearly six hours uninterrupted the first night I used his tips.

Just as Dr. Ashley advised, I was almost always militant about my sleep ritual. When I did stay up too late, ate too much before bed, or missed several workouts at the gym, my brain paid for it. My sleep quality diminished and I woke up multiple times in one night. As a result, my head burned and my memory was worse during the day. Only when I resumed following his tips did the symptoms subside.

However, regardless of how religious I was about my ritual, I still never slept more than six hours in one night (usually it was five hours), and I never felt quite rejuvenated. I rarely made it through the day without at least two short naps, and I still planned daily events around my sleep schedule. For example, if I was invited to an evening social function and it was the same day I worked at my part-time job, I needed a nap or I'd be too exhausted to attend. If I did find the time for a nap, it meant I wouldn't sleep well at night, and feel miserable the following day. It was like a never-ending torture cycle.

I did the best I could to control my sleep disorder until I decided to give in and see if a prescribed medication could help. Admittedly, I hadn't been good about having an annual physical exam since I moved to Utah, which meant I hadn't talked to a general practitioner about my brain injury or my sleep disorder. My New Year's Resolution was to change this, and make an appointment with a doctor.

At the exam, she performed all the routine tests, such as thyroid, cholesterol, and blood, before asking me, "Do you have any other issues or concerns?" I slid right into my answer, without hesitation, which amazed me since normally my thoughts vanished midsentence whenever I talked about my accident.

"Well, I was severely injured in a car accident back in 1994, I fractured both femurs, my neck, and I have a Traumatic Brain Injury," I explained, as I pointed directly to the smile on my forehead. "The worst part is that I have this terrible sleep disorder. I mean good sleep-hygiene helps, but I still have to plan my life around my sleep schedule."

"Have you ever participated in a sleep study?"

"No, what's that?" I asked. "I haven't done anything other than try to go to bed at the same time every night, and sleep with an eye mask and ear plugs," I explained. "Plus, I eat healthy and exercise regularly."

"Well, it's officially called Polysomnography. The test is used to diagnose, or rule out, many types of sleep disorders including narcolepsy, restless legs syndrome, REM behavior disorder, parasomnias, and sleep apnea."

"Sleep apnea? Are you kidding me? I don't have that!"

"How do you know, Jennifer?"

Maybe I don't know, I thought. Her question surprised me. "Well, wouldn't I know if I stopped breathing?" As much as I'd tried to control my disorder, I didn't sleep well at night, so maybe there was something else going on.

"Many of these disorders are common with a brain injury. Very often, people who sleep alone don't know if they stop breathing briefly in the middle of the night, but they're waking up so much, they never feel rested. I want to send you to Intermountain Sleep Disorders Center here in Salt Lake," she told me.

Less than one month later, I participated in a sleep study with Dr. John Krueger, and the results changed everything for me. I slept over night at the hospital, attached to a bunch of wires that measured my breathing, heart rate, and leg movement during sleep. Just as I expected, the doctor didn't find signs of sleep apnea or restless leg syndrome. But, he did find that only 16% of my sleep was spent in Rapid Eye Movement or REM, and normal is 20-25%. This, he said, was directly due to my Traumatic Brain Injury, which explained why I never felt rested during the day.

My doctor prescribed a sleep aid and the first night I used it I slept blissfully, uninterrupted for eight hours. Most importantly, I didn't need a break or a nap at any point during the following day, which was something I hadn't experienced even once since my injury. The difference a few lifestyle changes, combined with the medication, made for me were miraculous. I slept deeper than I had in years. My eyes looked brighter, my memory was sharper, and for the first time in over fourteen years, I felt exactly like the Jennifer I was supposed to be.

19

Note to Self: Stop Sprinting

Physical activity is like cognitive candy.

~John Medina

Dr. Glen Johnson[4], clinical neuropsychologist, once said that having a Brain Injury is like running a marathon. A marathon is 26 miles, but you can't sprint for 26 miles. You have to pace yourself for the long race and keep as positive an attitude as you can. For years after my injury, I was stuck in the last leg of the race, doing a terrible job trying to keep up when I wasn't prepared to be running a marathon in the first place. I constantly wrestled with feelings of frustration that my life was changed because of a car accident.

After learning more about Traumatic Brain Injury, I now realize there is nothing I can do to control the fact that TBI affects me, but I can control *how* it affects me. I do this by maintaining strict sleep hygiene, eating a healthy diet, and

---

[4] Dr. Glen Johnson offers a free online book providing information on Traumatic Brain Injury (TBI) in clear, easy-to-read language, located at www.tbiguide.com.

exercising regularly. The combination of these three elements is essential. Of course, it's important for anyone recovering from an injury to obtain medical clearance before beginning exercise, but committing myself to a regular fitness routine at my local health club, especially yoga, has changed the way I handle my life.

Good health and exercise have always been part of my lifestyle. My injury distorted this. Before high school, I was an amateur competitive figure skater, and I played soccer and basketball during high school. I can't remember a time when my parents and I weren't regulars at our local health club. Before the accident, I religiously attended step aerobics class, and the first time I tried this after my injury, I tripped five times in one class; probably because I still experienced vestibular problems. Nevertheless, I stopped doing step aerobics.

Shortly after I moved to Utah, I started browsing through the magazine *Yoga Journal* while waiting in line at the grocery store. It had several articles claiming yoga could melt away anxiety, calm a reactive mind, and balance energy. I think it even had one about how yoga helped some people recover from an injury. I was willing to try anything that might improve my physical balance, help me sleep better, and not worry so much about the way my injury was affecting me. I also wondered if stretching might alleviate the scar tissue in my legs.

I didn't know much about yoga, and I assumed only granola-types or hippies did it. I imagined myself practicing while seated on the floor with crossed legs, hands in prayer position, and chanting monosyllabic words; which seemed silly, but I didn't care. I just wanted to feel better and fix my brain injury. One week later I went to a local studio to give yoga a try.

My first class was much harder than I'd expected. There were a lot of people in the class, and I assumed they'd all been practicing for years. Clearly, I was the most inflexible person in the room. The instructor had us bend our bodies in confusing poses which irritated the scar tissue in my thighs, aggravated my double vision, and challenged my balance. *If he only understood the effects of my injury, then he'd never expect me to do these ridiculous poses*, I thought. *But, I'll just do the best I can.*

I've since learned that there are many different styles of yoga, and it's not just about stretching. In one pose, I was asked to stand on my left leg, draw my right foot up off the floor, take hold of my right ankle with my right hand, straighten my leg and stay balanced like this. I'd seen magazine pictures of people gracefully holding poses, but with the studio's wall-to-wall mirrors, I knew I didn't look like this. My balancing leg wobbled as my right knee shook. I couldn't even hold on to my foot for more than two seconds because it was greased with so much sweat.

"Next we'll do Tree Pose," the instructor said, as he guided us how to balance on one foot with the other leg almost resting in our crotch, our hands in prayer position. Without my arms to help me balance, I couldn't even get my foot to my thigh, so I just rested it on my knee.

"Avoid your knee," he warned. "If it's not in your practice today, just rest your foot at your ankle, like this," and he showed us a modified pose. I stared at myself in the mirror, barely balancing in my modified pose, thinking how much a TBI required modification in everything. I hated that I felt so different.

But, then I looked at the woman to my left and saw her foot resting at her ankle too. The man to my right rested his foot a little higher than us, above his ankle, but certainly nowhere near his thigh, and the man in front of me had his leg perfectly positioned at his thigh. Everyone practiced at different levels.

"Maybe a full Tree Pose is not in your practice today," the teacher told us, "and that's okay." He spoke to the entire class, but it seemed like he looked directly at me. My foot fell from my ankle because I focused on what he'd just said. I repeated his words in my mind. *Maybe it's not in my practice today, and that's okay. Maybe it's not in my practice today, and that's okay.*

I watched another woman rest on the floor in Child's Pose, rather than do Tree Pose with everyone else, so I copied her in this simple position. "If you ever feel you need a break from our practice, you can always rest in Child's Pose," the instructor explained. "This pose helps relieve stress and fatigue, and calms the brain. I see a few of you doing that now, and I think it's great."

I knew I should be focusing on my own practice, but as I rested in Child's Pose, I couldn't stop thinking about the instructor's words, "…not in your practice today, and that's okay." I realized that yoga was not about focusing on which poses I couldn't do, but on those I could.

I have a brain injury, is that okay too? I knew I'd been wasting my already depleted energy on negative thoughts about my injury, which was something I could not change. I decided to add to his phrase, and told myself, "Maybe it's not in my practice today *because I have a brain injury,* and that's okay." My purpose in yoga was not to measure my success by looking at someone else, but by challenging myself according to my own limitations. The same concept applies to my life with a Traumatic Brain Injury.

When I left the studio that night, I drove home feeling surprisingly sweaty, but toxin-free. It was as if I had been liberated from the heavy-laden, negative thoughts about myself and my injury. I loved how I felt, so I returned to yoga the next day, three times the following week, and three times during the next week.

After my eighth practice, I was able to rest my foot at my thigh during Tree Pose. I didn't balance in this position for long, but I also didn't look around at where everyone else in the class had their foot positioned. This was my own battle, and I felt at peace because finally I understood the concept of accepting myself unconditionally. Comparatively, a Traumatic Brain Injury had handed me a set of challenges, and I needed to stop comparing my post-injury abilities to my pre-injury abilities. My new goal was simply to try and progress from my present level.

I now have my own subscription to *Yoga Journal* and every issue includes at least one article that helps me manage my injury. The October 2008 issue had an article called "Good Memory," which discussed how yoga and exercise can improve your memory by enhancing your focus. According to recent studies published in *Science* and in the *Journal of Neuroscience*, exercise can stimulate the generation of new brain cells and help cells to migrate from one area of the brain to another. It's neurogenesis.

Swami Muktananda[5] describes a yogi as a person who knows how to turn every circumstance of life to her advantage because she takes whatever material life throws. Yoga and fitness has become my new outlet for control. It's something I can do to challenge both my mind and my body. As I do so, I feel better. I sleep deeper, my memory is sharper, and I can now balance a little longer on one foot in Tree Pose.

---

[5] Swami Muktananda (1908-1982) was the founder of Siddha Yoga, a new religious movement based on the Hindu philosophy of Kashmir Shaivism.

20

Note to Self: Remember Dr. Tom White Dinner

Memory is deceptive because it is colored by today's events.

~Albert Einstein

I often forget about the smile on my forehead; this scar has become a part of my face now. However, not a day goes by that I don't think about the scars inside my head. When I struggle with sleeplessness, or when I forget the names of close friends, or when I read the first five pages of my book club assignment for the fifth time, and I can't remember what I've read, I really hate my injury. But, these are just brief moments, requiring accommodations and acceptance. Every day I learn again how to accept my injury.

Dr. White did his surgical training at the University of Utah and since his wife, Sheri, was raised in the state, I wondered if they ever came to see family and friends. I had Dr. White's contact information, so I sent him an email in hopes that we could arrange a meeting.

In the email, I told him I was now happily living in Utah. "The move was a good decision for me," I explained. I made sure he knew I would love to see him the next time he was in town. He sent a response almost immediately.

"Thanks for the note, Jennifer. It's great to hear from you because we will actually be in Utah next month!" A short cyberspace conversation followed, and I set up a time and place to meet Dr. White, Sheri, and their kids for dinner. I invited Brent and his family to come along.

I wanted to interview Dr. White and get his impressions of my recovery. *What were the doctors thinking when I first arrived at the hospital? Did he think I'd die? Why did I survive such serious injuries?* I had so many questions after reading my mom's journals and seeing photographs of myself just after the accident.

On February 18, 2006, 4991 days after my accident, Brent, Kimberly, their kids and I packed into their minivan to meet Dr. White and his family for dinner at an Italian restaurant in Salt Lake. We pulled up right on time for our 6:00 P.M. reservation. My heart pounded with excitement as I stepped out of the car. I'd seen him only twice since my discharge from Regional West Medical Center; once when I went to Nebraska in May of 1995 to visit the hospital staff, and once a few years later in Minneapolis when he came to golf with some of his friends. This time I had a list of questions to ask about my injury. Knowing I'd forget his answers, I brought a tape recorder and microphone.

Although the White family had not yet arrived at the restaurant, the hostess seated us right away upstairs. Just after we got to our table, Kimberly said she had to use the bathroom, so I decided to follow her downstairs to the lobby and wait for the Whites.

"I'm sure they can figure out where we are, Jennifer" Brent said. But, I was excited and wanted to see him right as he came into the restaurant. I imagined Dr. White walking in: we'd see each other, our eyes would meet, and then I'd run up to give him a big hug. This is exactly how it did happen.

He and his family followed me upstairs to our table. "Dr. White, sit here next to me, so I can interview you about the accident," I directed, pointing to the tape recorder as I attached a little microphone to his shirt collar.

"Do I need my attorney present?" the doctor asked, in jest.

"No!" I giggled. "I really want to know what happened to me under your care at the hospital. I want to know what you think about my accident and my recovery." The waiter came and we ordered our food.

"Dr. White," I started to ask my first question, but then I paused. "I call you Dr. White because that's how my family always refers to you," I explained.

He smiled, "Yes, going forward, let's just forget the formal titles. My name is Tom."

I grinned and felt a little embarrassed. Dr. White hadn't officially been my doctor for almost twelve years, so I guess it was time to call him by his first name. I pressed the record button on my tape recorder.

"Okay, *Tom*," I asked. "Do you remember when you first saw me?"

"Yes, I remember. We put you on the gurney and started looking you over. You were one banged-up girl. I don't believe you had a breathing tube at that point, so we went ahead and secured your airway. I remember seeing a big dramatic scalp laceration, with an exposed skull. It was pretty dramatic. I remember you had bilateral femur fractures, and they were open. I remember your feet were deformed and bent, with open fractures on your toes. I remember we sent you to the CAT scan and scanned your head and neck, your abdomen and chest and you had fractures in your neck: C1 and C2."

"Did you think I'd die?" I frankly asked.

"No," he answered. "But, I knew you were critically injured. I thought there was a good chance you would make it because the best thing was that there wasn't obvious hemorrhage or a bunch of diffused bleeding on your brain. You were in a coma and you had a bad head injury, but it wasn't a head injury requiring immediate operation. You were pretty banged up, but I didn't think you were going to die, I mean, I hoped you wouldn't!"

I laughed out loud when he said this. I don't know why his comment struck me as so funny.

"Things happen!" Tom said, with medical realism.

"That's true!" I nodded. We were all hoping I wouldn't die. Just then my niece, Rachel, climbed onto my lap. I hugged her and pointed to Dr. White.

"This is Tom White," I explained. "He has something to do with this." I touched the scar on my forehead and asked Rachel, "What is this?"

"A smile!" she exclaimed, smiling herself.

"Yes, you definitely have two smiles," Dr. White assured me.

"So, Tom," I continued with my interview, "do you remember a lot about my injuries?"

"I remember a fair amount of it, yes. It doesn't seem like just yesterday, but I can remember a lot of it."

"So, then do you remember exactly when I came into the hospital? You were there?" I asked. My voice rose slightly as I spoke because my three-year-old nephew, Charlie, who sat on his dad's lap, banged his fork loudly against his plate.

"I was on trauma call when the accident happened. I don't remember what time of day it was and—"

Just then I interrupted Tom as I pleaded with Charlie to stop making noise, "Stop banging your fork, Charlie!" My brain injury has left me with little tolerance for loud noises. I then looked at Tom, hoping he'd finish his sentence.

"I don't recall whether I came in from home, or if I was already at the hospital, but I know I was at the emergency room when you arrived. We got word that you were coming up from Kimball. They did your initial stabilization and resuscitation and then they sent you up to us, I believe by helicopter, in fact I believe you came by military helicopter."

"Do you remember when you first saw me?" I asked, forgetting I had already asked this question. I caught myself and rephrased the question. "I mean—wait—I mean, do you remember the first time you met my mom, when she was on the helicopter with me?"

"Your mom?" he questioned, with a confused look.

"Well, yes, my parents, they were with me in the helicopter right?"

"No, Jennifer, no, they were in Minnesota."

"Huh? No, my mom…she was there!" I paused and turned to my brother for clarification. "Brent, Mom was still in Minnesota when I first got to Scottsbluff?"

"Yeah, Jennifer, they were still in Minnesota until about ten o'clock. I was in Utah. No family was there with you at first."

My heart dropped. "I was all alone?" I asked this question again for confirmation. It seems obvious now, but at the time, I'd heard so many of my mom's hospital stories, that I never made the connection she wasn't with me at first.

"Yeah, you were all by yourself," Tom answered my question. "Well, you had us!"

We both smiled. "I guess I wasn't completely alone as I had the doctors and nurses at Regional West caring for me!"

Charlie banged his fork against Brent's water glass again, and I could hear restaurant chatter from the table next to ours so clearly that I almost couldn't hear my own thoughts. I leaned my head forward, closer to the recorder, afraid the noise would prevent the microphone from catching my words. My head started spinning, so I tried hard to focus on the conversation.

Tom continued, "Your parents needed some positive information to hold on to, and that was my job. Plus, I believed you had a good chance."

"You did? Why? Why did you believe it?"

"Just because you were young and you were healthy and, ah, I don't know. I don't know…I was…I was optimistic. Yeah, I guess I can't explain that, I had a…a—"

"Gut feeling?" I interrupted.

"Yeah, I think it was a gut feeling, and also I think it's unfair to predict about my patients, either positively or negatively, because if you do that, I think you develop a bias on how you are going to treat the patient. If you think they are going to do poorly, then it can influence how you take care of them; it does for me anyway, so I try to avoid that."

Just then two waiters brought our food. "Can we take a break?" Tom asked. I pressed the pause button on the recorder and our conversation ended for a while. I couldn't think of any more questions anyway.

When everyone finished gorging themselves on chicken, pasta and other Italian fare, Tom turned to me, "So, now let me ask you some questions!" he asked. *Oh this is good.* Curious to hear what he'd ask, I pressed the record button again. "What's the first thing you remember after the accident? Do you even remember the accident first of all?"

"No, nothing," I answered. "I remember nothing about being in Nebraska. I do remember leaving for college that year. I remember completing a study abroad in Chile, spending the summer at home in Minnesota, and then feeling anxious to return to BYU at the end of the summer. After that, my memory is empty until about the first week in November when I have some memories from the hospital in Minnesota. I remember feeling irate, punching nurses, trying to pull off my Halo Brace. I remember being irritated that I was in the hospital."

It felt so great to say all this to a doctor who fully understood the severity of my injury. "The thing is," I continued, "when I first went back to college, I had to talk about my car accident several times a day. Sometimes I felt like everyone was staring at me, asking about my scars. I constantly felt like I had to explain myself, and apologize for my bad memory. I tried to mask my injury, and pretend that life looked the same as it did before when inside I felt pretty disconcerted. And you know, you try to get past it," I explained. "I've really tried to accept my condition, and know that I can still be a successful person. Success by my new standards has little to do with how much I achieve. More importantly, I know that I can still be a happy person."

Tom nodded in agreement. "I have another question," he asked. "When did you feel like you were healed from a physical standpoint? How long did it take for all the bone pain, hip pain and soreness to go away? When was all that normal again?"

"That's a great question," I responded. "I really don't think I'm 100% recovered, but I think I'm as recovered as I'll ever get, and I don't think this happened until I moved to Utah over two years ago. So, that would make my recovery nine years."

I spoke quickly, so I wouldn't forget what I was saying before getting everything out. "A year before I moved to Utah, I worked full-time while attending graduate school. I had big plans to further my education, to travel a lot. I wanted to accomplish things, and achieve my goals. But, I was just so tired all the time, kind of in a daze, and I just, I just couldn't handle that life."

"So you reset your expectations at some point?" Tom asked, nodding.

Clearly he understood. "Yes! And that happened only a couple years ago. Yep, life has slowed down for me now, and I'm really taking care of myself. I've found a great part-time job. I exercise at the gym several times per week. I take rest breaks every day. I spend time with my nieces and nephews. Life is good. I mean, if I could go back in time and change the events of August 23rd, 1994, I certainly would, because I wouldn't wish a Traumatic Brain Injury on anyone. But you know, Tom, I don't have that option, so I choose to accept what happened and embrace my injury."

With a big smile on my face, and another smile on my forehead, I felt ready to turn the recorder off.

Photographs

My 1987 Mitsubishi, Montero after the accident.

**Outside at Regional West Medical Center with Dad, Mom, and
Brent, about three weeks after the accident.**

Me, Tom and Sheri White, together at dinner in 2006.

Me, 14 years post-injury, practicing yoga.

Epilogue

I have good days and bad days. A good day means I don't feel like a metal bar has shot through my head, and I have a healthy amount of physical energy. My brain doesn't hurt, and I feel like the old me, like the woman I'm supposed to be.

Typically, a good day happens when I've been relentless about my brain injury management strategies. If I say "no" to an activity because I'm exhausted, it can be a good day. When I get enough sleep at night, it can be a great day. I sleep well when, in addition to taking my prescribed sleep medication, I go to bed at the same time every night, exercise in the morning, and eat clean. Eating clean means I consume mostly complex carbohydrates, protein, fruits and vegetables. I avoid sugar, too much salt and refined carbohydrate foods such as white rice and pasta made with white flour. I try to do cardio and weight bearing exercises every other day, with a yoga practice on alternate days. I have good days when I stick to my commitment to control my brain injury rather than let it control me.

A bad day means I'm cognitively exhausted, and I only want to be alone in a quiet, dark room. This happens when I have not been strict about my strategies. It also happens when I travel long distances, after I face a large group of unfamiliar people, or enter a large shopping mall without a plan. It's consistently a bad day if I let myself stay up too late, or when I waste energy thinking things like, *the pre-injury Jennifer wouldn't tire out like that*, or *the pre-injury Jennifer would remember that*. My head and heart feel awful when I compare the old me to the new me.

I used to search for ways to restore my old self, and to do things in the same ways as I did them before my injury. But then I remember what my mom once told me, "Maybe this is what you're supposed to learn from your accident, Jennifer, that you can't control everything. Sometimes unexpected things happen and you must discover ways to rise above them."

She was absolutely right. As soon as I began embracing my brain injury, rather than ignoring it, the sooner I stopped hating my life.

I made the most progress with this after becoming involved in the brain injury community. The Brain Injury Association of Utah Family and Professionals Conference taught me how to manage my injury. Regular attendance at a brain injury support group helps me understand that my experience is not unique. Reading other books written by other survivors or their family members validates my struggle, and I learn how others do it. I'm past feeling angry about my injury because I recognize a positive outcome. My experience has made me more resilient in other difficult situations. I'm more patient with myself and with others, especially those who are struggling to overcome a difficulty. Most importantly, I'm emotionally stronger now because I know I can handle almost anything if I'm able to manage my life with a Traumatic Brain Injury.

CPSIA information can be obtained at www.ICGtesting.com
Printed in the USA
LVOW060116050113

314347LV00001B/320/P

9 780578 013046